CARL SCHMITT
&
LEO STRAUSS

T0373382

HEINRICH MEIER

CARL SCHMITT
&
LEO STRAUSS
The Hidden Dialogue

Including Strauss's Notes on Schmitt's
Concept of the Political
& Three Letters from Strauss to Schmitt

TRANSLATED BY J. HARVEY LOMAX

FOREWORD BY JOSEPH CROPSEY

THE UNIVERSITY OF CHICAGO PRESS
CHICAGO AND LONDON

The University of Chicago Press, Chicago 60637
The University of Chicago Press, Ltd., London
© 1995 by The University of Chicago
All rights reserved. Published 1995
Paperback edition 2006
Printed and bound by CPI Group (UK) Ltd, Croydon, CR0 4YY
12 11 10 09 08 07 06   2 3 4 5
ISBN-13: 978-0-226-51889-3 (cloth)
ISBN-13: 978-0-226-51888-6 (paper)
ISBN-10: 0-226-51888-4 (paper)

Originally published as *Carl Schmitt, Leo Strauss und "Der Begriff des Politischen": Zu einem Dialog unter Abwesenden*, ©1988 J.B. Metzlersche Verlagsbuchhandlung und Carl Ernst Poeschel Verlag GmbH in Stuttgart.

Library of Congress Cataloging-in-Publication Data

Meier, Heinrich, 1953–
    [Carl Schmitt, Leo Strauss und "Der Begriff des Politischen". English]
    Carl Schmitt and Leo Strauss : the hidden dialogue ; including Strauss's notes on Schmitt's Concept of the political and three letters from Strauss to Schmitt / Heinrich Meier ; translated by J. Harvey Lomax; foreword by Joseph Cropsey.
       p.   cm.
    Includes index.
    1. Schmitt, Carl, 1888–   Begriff des Politischen.   2. Strauss, Leo—Correspondence.   3. Schmitt, Carl, 1888–   —Correspondence.   4. Political science.   5. State, The.   I. Title.
JA74.S33M413   1995
320—dc20   95-8803
                                                          CIP

To Harvey C. Mansfield
dedicated by the translator

CONTENTS

TRANSLATOR'S ACKNOWLEDGMENTS

The Lynde and Harry Bradley Foundation generously supplied the financial assistance necessary to prepare this translation for publication. The translator gratefully acknowledges Dr. Hillel Fradkin and the Board of the Bradley Foundation both for their kind moral support and for the munificent grant.

The Department of Political Science of the University of Memphis also deserves acknowledgment for providing the translator a leave of absence to make possible the completion of the present volume.

FOREWORD

The animating theme of the discourse between Carl Schmitt and Leo Strauss is "the political." What is "the political"? What distinguishes the political from every other human association, modality, or enterprise? Schmitt proposed an answer to the question that was provocative to the point of appearing perverse. Whereas according to an understanding that could claim to be self-evident, political society exists to promote peace among men, Schmitt argued that the essence of the political is polemic. He did not mean that there is a tragic defect in the ground of our being that condemns us forever to internecine hatred, and to give effect to that hatred with a higher efficiency by organizing ourselves in polities. Much to the contrary, he argued that the human beings are divided, and woe to them if they should ever cease to be divided, over the issues that go to the heart of humanity's existence. The beasts fight and kill in order to satisfy the lowest craving, which is for preservation. It belongs only to human beings to make war, not only to kill but to die, for a high cause and ultimately for the highest cause, which is their faith. Schmitt can agree with those who have perceived the human record as a history of bloodshed, but far from interpreting the fact as a sign of God's neglect or punishment, he sees it as an evidence of God's providence. By a dialectic of conflict, of "ideals" that men take seriously enough to contend over, and not by any mere dialectic of reason, mankind is preserved from the lassitude of indifference that is the soul's death.

Schmitt's own mortal enemy is liberalism, which he demonizes as the pacifistic, all-tolerating, rationalist-atheist antithesis of "the political" conceived as he defined it. Liberalism is thus complicitous with communism in standing for the withering away of the political and replacing it with the technological—the reduction of humanity to the last man. The skeleton of Schmitt's ideology exposes the shape not only of his own but of his contemporary Heidegger's adherence to the National Socialist party. It accords with Heidegger's famous 1935 (and 1953) remark in praise of the "inner truth and greatness" of National Socialism, on the basis of which he could consign the American and Soviet Unions alike to identical moral obloquy.

Schmitt's theory of the political was the obverse of his critique of liberalism. Strauss engaged him on the field of the political, the more comprehensive and presumably the primary category. Strauss saw that if Schmitt applauded strife itself as humanizing simply because it preserves mankind from the moral torpor of the technological terrarium, then Schmitt was no better than the value-free liberals he condemned, for both he and they admitted any end as equally choiceworthy with any other. Schmitt might stipulate for a higher, i.e., a more violent, commitment to the adopted value, read "faith," but Strauss made it clear that that would be a distinction without a significant difference. On the other hand, if Schmitt escaped the stigma of crypto-liberal relativism by positing religious faith as the absolute object of the commitment that defines the political and inspires men to kill and die, then Strauss was there to rejoin that nature, especially human nature, was a more primordial category than faith. The definition of the political should then be elicited from the ground of nature, as philosophers had been seeking to do from antiquity on.

The dialogue recorded and explicated here so ably by Dr. Heinrich Meier occurred in the few years immediately preceding the collapse of liberal democracy and the advent of its antithesis in Germany. The manifest vulnerability of the infant Weimar Republic would by itself have been sufficient, without the influence of Nietzsche and of other endemic antidemocratic social forces, to stimulate speculation on the nature of the liberal polity. As Schmitt was the first to acknowledge, and as the reader will see, Strauss's critique of Schmitt's book deepened that speculation at the same time that it carried Schmitt's own meaning into a clearer light than Schmitt himself had managed to do.

Dr. Heinrich Meier has brought to this book an expert's familiarity with the thought of Schmitt and Strauss, with special emphasis on the relation of theology and politics that is known to have preoccupied both men. In full awareness that the so-called theological-political problem implicates the even larger issue of the relation between reason and revelation, Dr. Meier has earned the reader's gratitude for the care and insight with which he has presented this exchange on a theme that can never lose its vital importance for our understanding of the way we live. As Dr. Meier makes abundantly clear, Carl Schmitt spoke in the name of an apprehension that liberal democracy might inherit the world. Now, in an epoch much affected by the end of the Cold War, such a consummation has been welcomed as the putative end of the history. Under all conditions, and especially our own, the political project for the emancipation and enlightenment of mankind in an atmosphere of comity and plenty will be a worthy object of intelligent inquiry. Dr. Meier has provided, in this book, a humane and scholarly impetus to such inquiry.

Joseph Cropsey

PREFACE TO THE AMERICAN EDITION

In the interim since this book was originally published in German in the spring of 1988, the debate over Carl Schmitt has changed profoundly. One critic who had perused the Schmitt literature of most recent vintage remarked not long ago that the present work has accomplished a "linguistic turn" and has given the increasingly animated discussion a new, "theological twist." This observation might be correct insofar as political theology has meanwhile moved emphatically and conspicuously into the center of attention. Political theology is central both to the appropriate interpretation of Schmitt's wide-ranging, circuitous oeuvre and to confrontation with what is truly in question in this interpretation. During the past seven years, the authors of numerous essays, monographs, and dissertations as well as countless articles and reviews have expressly or silently adopted as their premise the interpretation of Schmitt as spokesman for political theology and have chosen that premise as the point of departure for all further discussion. What explains the growing interest in Schmitt's political theology?

Let us begin with what is obvious. The context of a body of thought cannot be appropriately understood so long as its unifying center has not been disclosed and pondered. Now what one finds in the center of Schmitt's thought is his faith in revelation. By his own understanding, Schmitt is a political theologian. Whoever wishes to confront Schmitt's thought seriously must therefore come to grips with Schmitt's political theology, must enter into the self-understanding of the political theologian so as not to miss the decisive question from the outset. The key role of political theology is demonstrated by the fact that only an interpretation that takes its bearings from political theology can render comprehensible what must otherwise appear highly disparate, enigmatic, and obscure, if not altogether inconsistent. Moreover, in the summer of 1991 an extensive, previously unknown work entitled *Glossarium: Aufzeichnungen der Jahre 1947–51* was published from Schmitt's literary remains; that volume reveals the center of Schmitt's thought and his fundamental distinction between friend and enemy much more clearly than did the writings that appeared during the author's lifetime. The reflections and observations that Schmitt wrote three decades before his death read like a posthumous confirmation of the interpretation on which my *Dialogue* is based. By invitation of the newsweekly *Der Spiegel* I wrote a review essay for the general public that appeared simultaneously with the *Glossarium;* in 1994 it was published in an English translation under the title "The Philosopher as Enemy: On Carl Schmitt's *Glossarium*" (*New School for Social Research, Graduate Faculty Philosophy Journal*, vol. 17, nos. 1–2, pp. 325–32).

Schmitt took up the concept of political theology so as to determine his own position in the conflict of faith. Prior to the 1922 publication of Schmitt's treatise *Politische Theologie: Vier Kapitel zur Lehre von der Souveränität*, the expression had always been used to describe the position not of oneself but of the other, the opponent, the enemy. The antagonism envisaged by Schmitt when he specified his position was the antagonism between authority and anarchy, faith in revelation and atheism, obedience to and rebellion against the supreme sovereign. But authority, revelation, and obedience—regardless of the ways in which Schmitt may have updated them—are the decisive traits of the *concern* of political theology as such, which certainly did not originate with Schmitt's theorizings. That concern is as old as faith in revelation, and measured in human terms it will remain in existence as long as faith in a God who demands obedience continues to exist. Thus, after Schmitt had given a positive, or affirmative, meaning to political theology, the concept, understood as a political theory or doctrine that claims to be founded on faith in divine revelation, could also be used as a concept of self-determination and self-description by political theologians who reject Schmitt's political options and do not share *his* faith. In that sense the concept has been used since 1922 by political theologians with conservative or liberal positions, with revolutionary or counterrevolutionary convictions, of Christian, Jewish, or Islamic confessions. The concept has come into its own, and the new interest aroused in "postmodern times" by Schmitt's political theology has its deepest ground in the rediscovery of a premodern possibility, in the return to an "eternal possibility."

Political theology is a concept that makes a distinction insofar as the determination of its intrinsic concern distinguishes political theology from political philosophy. The two are not distinct in the way that two scholarly disciplines or two relatively independent domains of human thought and action can be distinguished from each other. Rather, they are divided by their insuperably opposed answers to

the question, *How am I to live?* That opposition establishes
an overall difference, in the way of life, in the positions on
morals, politics, revelation, and history. In the confrontation with political theology, political philosophy can therefore gain clarity about its own concern. The present dialogue serves such a clarification. It is a dialogue about the
difference between political theology and political philosophy. It therefore deals with political theology *and* political
philosophy, just as the book treats Carl Schmitt *and* Leo
Strauss. As far as I can tell, the reception of the book
thus far in Germany, as well as in France and Japan where
translations appeared in 1990 and 1993 respectively, has
concentrated almost exclusively on one side of the dialogue, namely on Schmitt and political theology. Perhaps
the publication of the American edition will bring greater
attention to the other side, Strauss and political philosophy.
The sequel and companion volume, *Die Lehre Carl Schmitts:
Vier Kapitel zur Unterscheidung Politischer Theologie und Politischer Philosophie*, which appeared in the autumn of 1994,
may also contribute to that end. *Die Lehre Carl Schmitts*
brings to a conclusion the confrontation that I began in the
present book.

In the fourth chapter of *Die Lehre Carl Schmitts* I discuss
in more detail the question of how Schmitt could believe,
in the "historical moment" of 1933 and later in retrospect
in 1945, that his decision in favor of Hitlerism could be
reconciled with his political theology. Further, the chapter
entitled "History, or The Christian Epimetheus" seemed
the proper place to discuss Schmitt's passionate hostility to
the Jews. But in the seventh chapter of *Carl Schmitt and
Leo Strauss* the attentive reader will discover the most important things to consider in both cases. Here I would simply add that the widely discussed "Case of Carl Schmitt"
will remain detoxified as long as Schmitt's political theol-

ogy is left out of account. The question raised by Schmitt's decision of 1933 in favor of the Third Reich has not been appropriately asked so long as it is addressed to Schmitt the "reckless adventurer" or "opportunist." The question must be aimed directly at Schmitt the political theologian. This approach is supported by the fact that political theologians Emanuel Hirsch and Friedrich Gogarten, Schmitt's theological friends Karl Eschweiler and Hans Barion, and Protestants like Paul Althaus and Gerhard Kittel made the same decision in 1933.

I close with two historical remarks. A few readers have assumed without further ado that Strauss had been informed about Schmitt's involvement with the Nazis when he wrote Schmitt the letter of July 10, 1933, from Paris that appears at the end of this book. We have no evidence whatsoever for this assumption. Rather, the exchange of letters with Jacob Klein suggests that Strauss knew nothing of the kind. His knowledge of Schmitt dating from the period before Strauss left Germany in late 1932 could hardly have led him to expect Schmitt's abrupt about-face after the Enabling Act of March 23, 1933.

After the German publication of my book, an old confidant of Schmitt, the jurist Günther Krauss, got in touch with me. In 1932–33 he had worked under Schmitt's supervision on a dissertation on the Protestant ecclesiastical lawyer Rudolph Sohm; later, Krauss was Schmitt's assistant at the University of Berlin. In 1988 he informed me that Schmitt, referring to Strauss's "Notes," had commented: "You've got to read that. He saw through me and X-rayed me as nobody else has."

Munich, February 1995   H.M.

PREFACE TO THE GERMAN EDITION

The present study was originally conceived as a contribution to a festschrift for Wilhelm Hennis. In that context it could have appeared only as a fragment. In its authentic form it is dedicated to Professor Hennis on his sixty-fifth birthday, February 18, 1988.

My special thanks go to Professor Joseph Cropsey of the University of Chicago. He has afforded me unlimited access to the literary estate of Leo Strauss, which is archived in the Special Collections Department of the University of Chicago Library, and he has supported my work in every way. With his kind permission the 1932 essay by Leo Strauss, which to the present day has remained the most significant confrontation with the *Concept of the Political*, is made available once again for the German reader.

The main points of the interpretation published here were first presented in the summer of 1979 to a group of young scholars in North Hessia. When seven years later I reexamined Carl Schmitt's oeuvre, Schmitt's thought appeared to me in the same light as it had earlier. But I believe I now see the center and the context of his thought more keenly, because I have a clearer view of the fundamental alternative.

Munich, October 1987   H.M.

CARL SCHMITT AND LEO STRAUSS:
THE HIDDEN DIALOGUE

But about what would a disagreement be, which we could not settle and which would cause us to be enemies and be angry with each other? Perhaps you cannot give an answer offhand; but let me suggest it. Is it not about right and wrong, and noble and disgraceful, and good and bad? Are not these the questions about which you and I and other people become enemies, when we do become enemies, because we differ about them and cannot reach any satisfactory agreement?

Plato, *Euthyphro* 7c-d
(trans. Harold North Fowler, 1926)

Carl Schmitt became more famous and more infamous through the *Concept of the Political* than through all his other works. That slim treatise[1] not only has connected the name of the author as closely as possible to the "distinction between friend and enemy" but has itself, unlike any other of Schmitt's writings, kindled such a distinction. The work has sown enmity and reaped enmity. Notwithstanding all his learned self-fashioning and his apologetic detoxification of his own remarks,[2] that result undoubtedly conformed to

1. Page numbers refer, unless otherwise indicated, to the following edition: *Der Begriff des Politischen. Text von 1932 mit einem Vorwort und drei Corollarien* (Berlin, 1963). Publications of Carl Schmitt are cited without mentioning the author.
2. In the 1963 Preface, Schmitt writes: "The text answers the challenge of an interim situation. The challenge that issues from the text itself is aimed primarily at experts on the constitution and jurists of international law." The "addressees" whom "the text primarily addresses" are "experts in the *jus publicum Europaeum*, experts in the history and present problems thereof" (13). Compare further the statement about the "defensive intermediate position" in which "the jurist of public law sees" himself (16) and the reference to the "original, informative purpose" of the text (16), the "individual sentences" of which, as Schmitt said in the 1932 Afterword, "are to serve scholarly discussions and exercises" (96). Arguing "purely juridically," Schmitt objects to the "reproach" that his concept of the enemy has primacy in the conception of the *Concept of the*

the political intention that determined Carl Schmitt's
course in his *Concept of the Political:* Schmitt confronts a
world that seeks to escape the distinction between friend
and enemy with the unavoidability of a radical Either-Or,
in order to make keener the "consciousness of the dire
emergency" (30)^{TN1} and to promote or reawaken the faculty that proves itself in "moments in which the enemy is
seen in concrete clarity as an enemy" (67); in an age in
which "nothing is more modern than the battle against the
political,"[3] his purpose is to bring to bear the "inescapability" of the political, the "inevitability" of enmity, even if
he should be the one who must face as their enemy all those
who want to know of no more enemies. The theoretician of
the political must be a political theoretician. A treatise
about the political can only be—of this conclusion Schmitt
is convinced—a political treatise, determined by enmity
and exposing itself to enmity.

How an essentially "political" discussion of the political
can be answered philosophically has been shown by Leo
Strauss. The answer does not involve withdrawing into the
unpolitical, screening out battle and decision, ignoring
friendship and enmity. The path Strauss takes in his
"Notes"[4] to Schmitt's *Concept of the Political* is that of radical

Political with the rejoinder "that every movement of a concept of law emerges
with dialectical necessity from negation. In the life, as in the theory, of the law,
the incorporation of negation is anything but a 'primacy' of what is negated. A
trial as a legal action only becomes thinkable at all when a law is negated.
Punishment and criminal law posit at their beginning not a deed but a criminal
misdeed. Does such positing perhaps reflect a 'positive' attitude toward criminal
misdeeds and toward a 'primacy' of crime?" (14–15).

3. *Politische Theologie. Vier Kapitel zur Lehre von der Souveränität* (Munich and
Leipzig, 1922), p. 55. (Second, revised edition, 1934, p. 82.)

4. The present volume includes a new translation of Strauss's essay, which
originally appeared as "Anmerkungen zu Carl Schmitt, *Der Begriff des Politischen*"
in *Archiv für Sozialwissenschaft und Sozialpolitik* (Tübingen), vol. 67, no. 6 (August–September, 1932), pp. 732–49. See the Editorial Note, page 120 below.
Citations to the Strauss essay on Schmitt refer to paragraphs, preceded by "N"

probing, going ever deeper, and bringing things to a climax, with the goal of driving the discussion to a confrontation over the very foundations of the political. The philosophical perspective does not prevent Strauss from grasping the "polemical meaning" that Schmitt's treatise, according to its own principles of understanding, is bound to have. On the contrary, this perspective enables Strauss to express the political-polemical intention of the text more clearly than Schmitt himself had done. At the same time, however, it protects Strauss from relying on what Schmitt presupposes as compelling and in need of no further foundation, namely, that *every* concept of the political must have a "concrete opposition in view" and be "bound to a concrete situation, the final consequence of which is a grouping into friends and enemies (which expresses itself in war or revolution)" (31). It is not apparent how this presupposition, or even the unquestioned acceptance of it as true, can be harmonized with a "pure and whole knowledge." Yet Schmitt puts the greatest hope in such knowledge—if indeed he does not claim it for himself. "From the power of a pure and whole knowledge," reads the solemn promise in which he has the book culminate, "arises the order of the human things" (95). Whatever the import of this order might be and wherever Schmitt's promise might find its final foundation, a pure and whole knowledge is, as Strauss rejoins to Schmitt, "never, unless by accident, polemical" (N34), and if it is to be whole and pure, and if it is to be *knowledge*, considered in human terms it can be achieved only by means of pure and whole questioning. Pure and whole questioning is radical questioning; radical questioning requires rigorously consistent thought. Resolute-

for "Notes"; in the present edition, paragraph numbers have been added in brackets.

ness and rigorous consistency of thought are successfully proven in thinking through the fundamental alternatives to the end, in uncovering the presuppositions of those alternatives, and in clarifying the problems involved. It is by radicalizing the questioning, by pondering philosophically the enigmatic appeal to a "pure and whole knowledge," that the "Notes on Carl Schmitt, *The Concept of the Political*" gain their superior argumentative power and their intellectual keenness.

Just as the *Concept of the Political* has an exceptional position among the works of Carl Schmitt, so are the "Notes" of Leo Strauss exceptional among the texts about Schmitt. Let us disregard what is most obvious and adhere to the authority of Schmitt. Taking a closer look, we find that the *Concept of the Political* holds its special position within Schmitt's oeuvre not only with respect to its object, to the way in which this object is treated, and to its influence. In yet another sense we are dealing with an exception. The *Concept of the Political* is the only text that Schmitt issued in three different editions.[5] It is the only text in which the

5. The first edition was published in the *Archiv für Sozialwissenschaft und Sozialpolitik* (Tübingen), vol. 58, no. 1 (September 1927), pp. 1–33, and reprinted unchanged in no. 5, *Probleme der Demokratie*, in the series *Politische Wissenschaft* (Berlin-Grunewald: Dr. Walther Rothschild, 1928), pp. 1–34. The second edition appeared as a separate publication under the title *Der Begriff des Politischen. Mit einer Rede über das Zeitalter der Neutralisierungen und Entpolitisierungen neu herausgegeben von* Carl Schmitt (Munich and Leipzig: Verlag von Duncker & Humblot, 1932), 82 pages. The text of the *Begriff des Politischen* appears on pages 7–65, and the revised version of "Die europäische Kultur in Zwischenstadien der Neutralisierung" (first published in *Europäische Revue*, vol. 5, no. 8 [November 1929], pp. 517–30) on pages 66–81. The third edition, *Der Begriff des Politischen* (Hamburg: Hanseatische Verlagsanstalt, 1933), contains 61 pages. "Das Zeitalter der Neutralisierungen und Entpolitisierungen" was not included in the third edition. On page 6 Schmitt writes: "The first edition of the *Concept of the Political* appeared in August 1927 in the *Heidelberger Archiv für Sozialwissenschaft und Sozialpolitik;* the second edition was published in October 1931 by Duncker und Humblot in Munich and Leipzig." Schmitt reissued the second edition in 1963 through Duncker und Humblot (see n. 1 above). The first sentence of the Preface reads:

changes are not limited to polishing style, introducing minor shifts in emphasis, and making opportunistic corrections, but reveal conceptual interventions and important clarifications of content.[6] And it is the only text in which, by means of significant deletions, elaborations, and reformulations, Schmitt reacts to a critique. Only in the case

---

"This reprint of the text on the 'Concept of the Political' contains the unaltered, complete text of the 1932 edition" (9). No reason is given for the reprint's containing not the final edition, which is in various respects superior, but the penultimate edition. Furthermore, that there was ever a third edition—not merely an "abridged" edition (as is occasionally asserted in the literature) but an altogether revised edition with many passages expanded and the content altered—remains unmentioned. The reason for Schmitt's silence, as well as for his decision to reprint "unaltered" the second rather than the third edition, is obvious: The text of 1933 was, because of several alterations and deletions that were "suited to the time," politically assailable in 1963 (pp. 13, 14, 22, 24, 25, 26, 44, 51; cf. on the other hand the new attack, "unsuited to the time," against euthanasia, p. 31). In 1963 the mention of National Socialism, a remark that was opportune in 1933, appeared to be inopportune ("The system of the Weimar coalition treated the National Socialists as illegal and 'unpeaceful,'" p. 30). And the anti-Semitic insinuations of the third edition were simply intolerable (cf. pp. 10, 44, 59, but above all p. 8, where Schmitt precedes a statement that has a scarcely concealed anti-Semitic thrust, about the "alien and the man who is of a different type," with a highly ironic appeal to Spinoza's *in suo esse perseverare*—without mentioning the philosopher by name).—The 1963 reprint reproduces the 1932 text verbatim; but Schmitt silently changed the division of paragraphs and of footnotes, the orthography, and the punctuation. Italics in the text are likewise added or omitted without being so marked (see n. 27 below). In all statements about the second edition I refer to the original of 1932. Page numbers, however, are indicated according to the 1963 reprint to facilitate reference for the reader. Page numbers that refer to the first edition of 1927 and the third of 1933 are preceded by I and III respectively.

6. Karl Löwith misses what is most important *for the substantial issue* when he declares: "The principle of *all* [Löwith's italics] changes within the various editions is . . . always the one occasionalism that characterizes Schmitt's situation-bound and therefore in each instance polemical decisions." Hugo Fiala (pseud.), "Politischer Dezisionismus," p. 119 n., in *Revue internationale de la théorie du droit—Internationale Zeitschrift für Theorie des Rechts*, Brünn, vol. 9, no. 2 (1935), pp. 101–23; republished with changes in 1960 under the title "Der okkasionelle Dezisionismus von Carl Schmitt" (*Sämtliche Schriften*, vol. 8 [Stuttgart, 1984]). Löwith mentions a total of three changes. They all concern the second and third editions. In the text (p. 119) he documents how Schmitt, "in a kind of toeing of the party line," deletes a statement about Marx, Lenin, and Lukács (62–63) and replaces it with an anti-Semitically sharpened attack on F. J. Stahl (III, 44).

of the *Concept of the Political* does Schmitt engage in a dialogue, both open and hidden, with an interpreter, a dialogue that follows the path of a careful revision of Schmitt's own text. The partner in the dialogue is the author of the "Notes," Leo Strauss. He is the only one among Schmitt's critics whose interpretation Schmitt would include, decades later, in a publication under Schmitt's name,[7] and Strauss is the only one Schmitt would publicly call an "important philosopher."[8] With these facts in mind, we need hardly evoke the judgment that Schmitt repeatedly ex-

---

In a footnote, Löwith refers just as aptly to a similar correction, no less "suited to the time," in the context of Schmitt's critique of Oppenheimer's view of the state (76–III, 59). The third change that Löwith mentions (p. 113 n.)—to be discussed below in detail—fills him with perplexity and surprises him, because it does not permit of explanation in terms of Schmitt's "political occasionalism." This alteration belongs to the modifications that point in the *opposite* direction, changes that Löwith does not perceive or does not want to acknowledge, and it can be understood appropriately only if one recognizes the dialogue in which the alteration provides an answer.

7. Strauss's essay is included in the American edition of *The Concept of the Political* (New Brunswick, NJ, 1976), edited by George Schwab, with whom Schmitt remained in close contact for decades. —Schmitt himself in 1932 had apparently seen to it that Strauss's "Notes" were published in the *Archiv für Sozialwissenschaft*, the same organ in which the *Concept of the Political* had appeared in 1927. In a letter dated June 10, 1932, to the head of the publishing house Duncker und Humblot Dr. Ludwig Feuchtwanger, a close acquaintance since World War I, Schmitt writes: "So far, perhaps a hundred reviews of the *Concept of the Political* have appeared, but I have learned little from them. The only item of interest is that Dr. Leo Strauss, the author of a book about Spinoza, has written a very good essay about my book—very critical, of course—which I hope to find a place for in Lederer's *Archiv für Sozialwissenschaft*." In a letter to Strauss of April 15, 1935, dealing with Strauss's just-published book *Philosophie und Gesetz*, Feuchtwanger remarks: "In 1932 the author of the *Concept of the Political* spoke to me about you with high esteem; but his praise was quite unnecessary, because I knew your book on Sp. . . . *I have high hopes for you as one of a very few who have something to say.*" —Schmitt's letter was made accessible to me by Prof. Helmut Quaritsch. I cite from it with permission of the owner of Duncker und Humblot, Norbert Simon. Feuchtwanger's letter is in the University of Chicago Library, Leo Strauss Papers, Box 1, Folder 13.

8. "Die andere Hegel-Linie. Hans Freyer zum 70. Geburtstag" in *Christ und Welt* (Stuttgart), July 25, 1957, p. 2. Schmitt refers to the dialogue between Leo Strauss and Alexandre Kojève in Strauss's book *De la tyrannie* (Paris, 1954).

pressed in conversations, that he knew of no one who understood him better than Strauss did with respect to the primary intention of the *Concept of the Political*. If we want to adhere to the authority of Schmitt, the judgment he indicated by his action, "by deed," is far more informative. The dialogue that Schmitt and Strauss held with one another in 1932–33 speaks a clear language. One must, of course, listen closely, for the second part of the dialogue is already a silent dialogue. A member of the Prussian State Council speaks to a "Jewish man of learning."[9] A Catholic teacher of constitutional law, whose political ambition has reached its zenith in Berlin and who has achieved the summit of his career, answers a still almost unknown young philosopher, who, in pursuit of intensive research on Hobbes, was driven in late 1932 by "a (in certain ways) gracious destiny"[10] to Paris and, several months later, to England, thanks in large part to benevolent support from the Berlin professor of law.[11] Who could be surprised, considering these circumstances, that in the 1933 edition of the *Concept of the Political* Schmitt never once mentions the name of his partner in dialogue, to whose published interpretation and privately reported questions[12] he replies?

---

9. *Der Leviathan in der Staatslehre des Thomas Hobbes. Sinn und Fehlschlag eines politischen Symbols* (Hamburg, 1938), p. 20. —In early July 1933, Schmitt was appointed by the Prussian prime minister, Hermann Göring, to the Prussian State Council. Schmitt had played a decisive role in the composition of the *Reichsstatthaltergesetz*[TN2] of April 1933 and had joined the National Socialist Party on May 1, 1933.

10. Leo Strauss, *Hobbes' politische Wissenschaft* (Neuwied, 1965), p. 8.

11. Schmitt wrote a professional evaluation of Strauss and his studies of Hobbes that contributed substantially to Strauss's receiving a grant from the Rockefeller Foundation in May 1932. The second evaluator was Ernst Cassirer, who had supervised Strauss's doctoral dissertation in 1921 in Hamburg. The grant was for a two-year residence for studies in France and England. (Leo Strauss Papers, Box 3, Folder 8.) See Strauss's letters of March 13, 1932, and July 10, 1933, pages 123, 127 below.

12. Letter of September 4, 1932, page 124 of this volume.

The political constellation in which the dialogue took place, the theoretical positions that collide here, the fundamental alternatives that become visible and are in question in this dialogue, the weight of the participants, their actions, and their mutual esteem—everything should command the reader's alert and patient attention to the dialogue between Schmitt and Strauss. Here is reason enough to follow the dialogue carefully and to enlist its aid in analyzing the *Concept of the Political*. Schmitt's eloquent silence in 1933 (about Strauss) and in 1963 (about the 1933 edition) speaks as little against such an approach as does the fact that the dialogue went altogether unnoticed in the literature on Schmitt that has long become extensive. *L'essence de la critique, c'est l'attention.*

I

Leo Strauss writes little about his contemporaries. With few does he expressly argue. He devotes detailed studies to only three theoreticians during their lifetimes; with only three does he enter into a public discourse or attempt to begin such a discourse—Alexandre Kojève, Martin Heidegger, and Carl Schmitt. Why Carl Schmitt? Why *The Concept of the Political*? What awakens, what kindles Strauss's special interest? Above all else, it is "the radical critique of liberalism that Schmitt strives for" (N26). It is a critique that Schmitt *strives for*, yet does not himself bring to a close. For the critique of liberalism that Schmitt *undertakes* is carried out and remains "in the horizon of liberalism." "His unliberal tendency" is obstructed "by the still unvanquished 'systematics of liberal thought'" (N35)—a systematics that, in Schmitt's own judgment, "despite all setbacks," has "still not been replaced by any other system in Europe today" (70). Put more precisely, what primarily interests Strauss in writing on the *Concept of the Political* is to complete the critique of liberalism.

This objective interest in the issue, which determines his entire confrontation with Schmitt's thought, leads Strauss not only to place himself into the orbit of Schmitt's strength but to make Schmitt's argument stronger at decisive points—and thus taken as a whole—than it really is. In face of the fundamental difficulty that besets Schmitt's undertaking in a liberal world, Strauss is glad to perform "the critic's duty to pay more attention to what distinguishes Schmitt from the prevailing view than to the respects in which he merely follows the prevailing view" (N6).

How strong Strauss makes Schmitt's position, and in what manner and with what intention he strengthens it, can be inferred from his interpreting Schmitt's theoretical approach as a whole and from the very beginning as an attempt to depart, in an original, logically rigorous, internally consistent way, from the liberal "philosophy of culture." Strauss explains Schmitt's point of departure—his understanding the question of the "essence of the political" (20, 45) from the outset as the question of what is *specific* to the political, and his demand for a *characteristic trait*, a *criterion*—not as resulting from indifference on Schmitt's part to the question of the genus within which the peculiarity of the political must be ascertained, but as deriving from a "deep suspicion of what is today the most obvious answer." Schmitt "pioneers a path to an original answer" "by using the phenomenon of the political to push the most obvious answer ad absurdum." But "what is still today, despite all challenges, the most obvious, genuinely liberal answer" tells us that this genus is "the '*culture*,' that is, the totality of 'human thought and action,' which is divided into 'various, relatively independent domains' [26], into 'provinces of culture' (Natorp)" (N7). The criterion of the political Schmitt specifies as the distinction between friend and enemy, whereby he expressly denies the homogeneity or analogy of that distinction to the "ultimate" distinctions of good and evil "in the domain of the moral," of beautiful and ugly "in the aesthetic domain," of useful and harmful "in the economic domain" (26). Thus his break with the conception of the liberal "philosophy of culture" is by no means limited to a particular "region." By conceiving the political as "independent" but "not in the sense of having its own new domain" (27), he is calling into question, if we are to understand him rightly, the doctrine of autonomous "provinces of culture" or "relatively independent domains." What is implied here, as Strauss emphasizes, is "a fundamental critique of at least the prevailing concept of culture" (N7). It must be granted that Schmitt "does not express" this criticism "everywhere. He too, using the terminology of a whole literature, occasionally speaks of the 'various, relatively independent domains of human thought and action' [26]." Because Strauss literally cited Schmitt's "occasionally" occurring expression only a few lines before in his elucidation of the liberal concept of culture, the seemingly casual indication of a logical inconsistency in the "expression" calls the reader's—and primarily Schmitt's own—attention to Schmitt's lack of clarity on an important point regarding the extent of his undertaking. In the 1933 edition of the *Concept of the Political,* the "relatively independent domains" are no longer anywhere to be found. Instead, Schmitt emphasizes by means of italics that the distinction between friend and enemy is *independent.* And, already in the opening section, the political opposition is now expressly contrasted to the oppositions between good and evil, beautiful and ugly, etc., as the "far deeper opposition."[13]

Strauss protects Schmitt from being misunderstood as "wanting, after liberalism has brought to recognition the autonomy of aesthetics, of morality, of science, of the economy, etc.," "now on his part to bring the autonomy of the political into recognition—in opposition to liberalism but nonetheless in continuation of the liberal aspirations for autonomy—the autonomy of the political." Although Schmitt expresses himself "in one passage" (71) in such a way "that a superficial reader" could get this impression, "the quotation marks that he places around the word 'autonomy' in the expression 'autonomy of the various do-

13. Cf. Strauss's critical remark in the second paragraph of his letter of September 4, 1932, page 124 below.

mains of human life' already show how little the foregoing is Schmitt's opinion." "Schmitt's aloofness from the prevailing concept of culture becomes fully clear," according to Strauss, "in the following indirect characterization of the aesthetic: 'the path from the metaphysical and the moral to the economic traverses the aesthetic, and the path across aesthetic consumption and enjoyment, be they ever so sublime, is the surest and most comfortable path to the universal economization of spiritual life . . .' [83]; for the prevailing concept of culture surely includes recognition of the autonomous value of the aesthetic—assuming that this concept is not altogether constituted precisely by that recognition" (N8). Schmitt answers this interpretation with slight alterations in the text, alterations that, slight as they are, signal assent no less clearly to his critic. In analogous fashion Schmitt immediately repeats five times, in the sentence that immediately follows the cited passage, the quotation marks that Strauss stressed at the beginning of his interpretation. Moreover, he adds a brief supplement that discernibly refers back to the statement with which Strauss closes: To liberalism it seems "altogether self-evident," Schmitt says in 1933, "that art is a 'daughter of freedom,' that aesthetic value-judgment is 'autonomous,' that artistic genius is 'sovereign,' *and that the work of art, 'being unbiased,' has its 'purpose in itself.'"[14]

14. III, 53, my emphasis. In 1932 the passage reads: "That art is a daughter of freedom, that aesthetic value-judgment is absolutely autonomous, that artistic genius is sovereign, seems self-evident to liberalism" (71). Schmitt made analogous changes in other passages. For example, "the norms or ideals of an economy that is thought to be autonomous" (49) becomes "the norms or ideals of an economy thought to be 'autonomously' self-regulating" (III, 31); and instead of "For the political opponents of a clear political theory it will therefore not be difficult to declare, in the name of any autonomous domain, that the clear knowledge and description of political phenomena and truths are immoral, uneconomical, unscientific, and above all—for politically this is crucial—devilry hors-la-loi that ought to be fought off" (65), the 1933 edition says: "He who is politically

One can speak of the sovereignty of artistic genius, and of the autonomy of the moral, the aesthetic, and the economic, as something self-evident only as long as the reality of the political is misunderstood, the opposition between friend and enemy is detoxified, and the exceptional case— which "here, as elsewhere," has a "significance that reveals the core of things" (35)—is made to fade from view. The peaceful coexistence of the "domains of human thought and action" is confounded by the "real possibility" of armed battle, a possibility that "belongs to the concept of the enemy" and constitutes the political (33). Though the individual may move in the various "provinces of culture" as a "free decision-maker," though he may seek or flee binding commitments there, consent to or disavow obligations, in the "sphere of the political" he encounters an objective, external force that affects him existentially, that makes a life-and-death claim upon him. He can "voluntarily die for whatever he wants to; that, like everything essential in an individualistic-liberal society, is altogether a 'private matter'" (49). On the other hand, the enemy, and war as the "most extreme realization of enmity" (33), confront him with a question that he cannot evade at will. They confront him with decisions in which he *must* decide about himself, in the face of which he is compelled to achieve clarity about his identity. For the political is located "not in fighting itself" but in a behavior that is oriented toward the real possibility of war, "in clear knowledge of one's own situation, defined by that possibility; and in the task of rightly distinguishing between friend and

---

interested in camouflages, concealments, and smokescreens therefore has a cakewalk. He need only defame, in the name of any 'autonomous domain,' the clear knowledge and description of political phenomena and truths as immoral, uneconomical, unscientific, and above all—for politically this is crucial—as devilry that ought to be fought off" (III, 46).

enemy" (37). In the face of war, the political question of rightly distinguishing between friend and enemy gains a gravity that raises the significance of that question far beyond the political. Strauss, in the following comment, expresses Schmitt's "unliberal tendency" with logical rigor: "War is not merely 'the most extreme political measure'; war is the dire emergency not merely within an 'autonomous' region—the region of the political—but for man, simply, because war has and retains a 'relationship to the real possibility of *physical killing*' [33]; this orientation, which is constitutive of the political, shows that the political is *fundamental* and not a 'relatively independent domain' alongside others. The political is the 'authoritative' [39]" (N9). In the very passage to which Strauss refers at the end of his formulation "The political is the authoritative,"[15] Schmitt in 1933 expands the text—in order to emphasize his opposition to the liberal "philosophy of culture" more pointedly than he had ever done before in the *Concept of the Political:* "The political unit," the text now reads, "is always, as long as it is present at all, the authoritative unit, total and sovereign. It is 'total' first because every matter can potentially be political and therefore can be affected by the political decision; and second because man is totally and existentially grasped in political participation. Politics is destiny."[16]

15. In the passage that Strauss cited as evidence, Schmitt had not spoken of the political as the "authoritative" but merely of the "authoritative human grouping," of the "authoritative unit," and of the "authoritative instance" (39). By contrast, in 1933, in another passage (III, 9) just as pertinent for the Straussian interpretation, he speaks anew of the "independence *and authoritativeness of the political opposition*" (my emphasis; cf. the wording in the second edition, 28).

16. III, 21. Schmitt altered the immediately preceding sentence in each of the three editions: "The political always determines the grouping that takes its bearings by the dire emergency" (I, 11). "The grouping that takes its bearings by the dire emergency is at any rate always political" (39). "The grouping that

II

The distance that Carl Schmitt covered on the way to the preceding statement was greater than a "superficial reader" of Strauss's essay might suppose. For Strauss also makes Schmitt's position appear stronger by avoiding any comment on the changes that Schmitt made between 1927 and 1932 in the conception of the *Concept of the Political.* If an attentive reader, induced by Strauss's single reference to a judgment by Schmitt on Thomas Hobbes that was modified in 1932,[17] should acquire the first edition and look at it more closely, he will find, upon perusal of it, that not only a "superficial reader could get the impression" that Schmitt wants "to bring the autonomy of the political into recognition, in opposition to liberalism but nonetheless in continuation of the liberal aspirations for autonomy." The alert reader will notice that, in the "one passage" in the 1932 edition that Strauss discusses in order to show "how little the foregoing is Schmitt's opinion," Schmitt in the first edition neither places the term "autonomy" in quotation marks nor proceeds to any open criticism of the "independence of aesthetic values" (I, 30). Finally, and most important, this reader will clearly perceive that Schmitt not only "occasionally" speaks of the "relatively independent domains of human thought and action" but expressly defines *the political itself* as a *domain,* "as one domain among others" (I, 3, 4), a definition that he just as expressly denies five years later (27, 38). Strauss doubtless has good reasons to overlook Schmitt's changes and to pass over in silence the contradictions of the book, which are

---

is determined by the dire emergency is at any rate always political" (III, 21). Cf., on details of the definitive version, the formulations in Strauss, N9 and N10.

17. Strauss's footnote to N14.

based upon "the history of its development." That Strauss
nevertheless, as elegantly and discreetly as possible, calls
attention to these things, is no less good a reason for us
briefly to consider Schmitt's initial conception and to examine more closely what Strauss, in his interpretation, leaves
undiscussed.

Schmitt begins his battle over the concept of the political
on the defensive. Against the negation of the political
by "the astonishingly consistent systematics of liberal
thought, a systematics that, despite seeming setbacks, still
definitely prevails today" (I, 29), he attempts to bring to
bear the "proper objectivity and independence of the political" (I, 5). His effort to obtain for the political the recognition that "every independent domain" (I, 3, 4) can claim
for itself and that liberalism does not deny to the "others"
(I, 29, 30) is defensive. His assertion that the distinction
between friend and enemy that is specific to the "domain
of the political" can "exist theoretically and practically
without moral, aesthetic, economic, or other distinctions being applied simultaneously" (I, 4), is defensive.
Schmitt's answer to the central question of the characteris-
tics of the political enemy—namely, that he is "plainly the
other, the alien" and that "to describe his essence" it suffices "that he is in an especially intensive sense existentially something other and alien, so that in case of conflict
he signifies the negation of one's own kind of existence
and therefore is fended off or fought in battle in order to
preserve one's own, proper kind of life" (I, 4)—is defensive. If for Schmitt the political is the thing to be defended
in an age of neutralizations and depoliticizations, then politics, in Schmitt's rhetoric, essentially appears to be defense. He speaks very insistently of *fending off* the enemy,
the "real" enemy, one's "own enemy" (I, 4, 9, 17, 29).
The enemy constantly makes his appearance as an at-

tacker; he never comes into sight, in the theoretical discussion, as the attacked. This perspective may distract the
reader from the question of how the "real enemy" can be
"known" and how one's "own, proper kind of life" is to
be maintained without "other distinctions being applied,"
without "normative prescriptions," "rational ends," "ideal
programs" coming into play. If the enemy attacks, the will
to ward him off is "fully self-evident" (I, 29). The enemy
defines himself as enemy by means of the attack; the reasons and motives of the enmity can then safely be ne-
glected as secondary, or so it may seem from the viewpoint
of the attacked. The rhetoric of the defensive, however,
not only helps Schmitt conceal theoretical difficulties in his
concept of the political. As a rhetoric of "pure politics,"[18]
his defensive rhetoric gives him the double political advantage of shielding his own "purely political" position against
all "normative" criticism and of simultaneously enabling
him to attack, with the superior self-certainty of the morally
indignant, any normative "intrusions" into and "encroach-
ments" upon the region of "pure politics": The enemy
who engages in politics in "an unpolitical and even antipolitical" guise violates the honesty and visibility of pure
politics. He deceives. He does not even shrink, for the
sake of his political advantage, from making himself guilty
of "high political abuse."[19] It is "something wholly self-

18. ". . . [I]f he adheres to his political thought with logical rigor, the theoretician of pure politics can discern even in the charge of immorality and cynicism
time and again only a political instrument of men concretely engaged in battle"
(I, 26). Previously Schmitt speaks of the "purely political concept" and of "purely
political thinkers" (I, 25). In 1932 all these statements have been altered (64,
65, 67).

19. I, 16, 20, 25, 26, 27, 32, 33. (Cf., in the second edition, 49, 55, 65, 66,
68, 76, 77.) Regarding Schmitt's high esteem for *honesty* and *visibility* in politics,
cf. "Wesen und Werden des faschistischen Staates" (1929), p. 114, and, further,
"Staatsethik und pluralistischer Staat" (1930), p. 143 (in *Positionen und Begriffe
im Kampf mit Weimar-Genf-Versailles 1923–1939* [Hamburg, 1940]), and *Staat, Be-*

evident" "that war is to be made only against a real enemy." The necessary physical fending off of a "real enemy
in the proper meaning" is "politically sensible," though
Schmitt does not hesitate to point out that this statement
is "not a legitimation or justification" but has "a purely
existential meaning" (I, 17). The situation is different as
soon as the enemy leaves the sphere of "pure politics"
and, "going beyond the political," depreciates "his enemy simultaneously in moral and other categories" and makes
him into "an inhuman monster that must be not only
fended off but definitively annihilated, and thus is no
longer even an enemy that can be treated objectively" (I,
9). Here the "real battle against a real enemy" falls into
the maelstrom "of ideal programs" or "normative prescriptions." However, as the moralist Schmitt knows, there is
"no rational end, no norm however right, no program however ideal, no legitimacy or legality that could justify human beings' killing one another over it." The defender of
pure politics continues: "If such a physical annihilation of
human life does not occur out of the proper assertion of
one's own form of existence against a likewise proper negation of this form, that annihilation plainly cannot be justified" (I, 17).

The rhetoric of pure politics, for all its political advantages for Schmitt, has a grave disadvantage. If Schmitt,
with his initial conception, succeeds in bringing to bear the
"proper objectivity and independence of the political," he

---

wegung, Volk. Die Dreigliederung der politischen Einheit (Hamburg, 1933), p. 28.
Decades later, Schmitt identifies by name the deepest ground of his abhorrence
of all invisible, anonymous powers that remain in concealment and make use of
veils when he speaks of a "Satanic temptation." "Nomos-Nahme-Name," in *Der
Beständige Aufbruch. Festschrift für Erich Przywara* (Nuremberg, 1959), p. 104. Cf.
"Die Sichtbarkeit der Kirche," in *Summa*, Zweites Viertel (Hellerau, 1917), pp.
71–80; and *Römischer Katholizismus und politische Form* (Hellerau, 1923), pp.
31–32, 39–40, 66. (2d ed., slightly altered [Munich, 1925], pp. 21, 26, 43.)

does so only at the price of reducing the political to foreign policy. "War is armed conflict between nations" (I, 6). Nations are the subjects of politics. Organized into political units, they constitute the "pluriverse" of the political world (I, 19). In 1927, domestic politics is mentioned almost exclusively with respect to foreign policy.[20] Conflicts in the interior of a state are discussed within the horizon of the question of what effects they could have on the capacity of the political unit to wage war (I, 9 ff.). Schmitt speaks of "war" seventy-seven times in the thirty-three paragraphs of his essay. The term "civil war" does not occur once. In 1931–32, Schmitt sees himself facing a changed political situation. The "systematics of liberal thought" has, to be sure, "still not been replaced by any other system," but it no longer "prevails." It no longer has a record of setbacks that are merely "seeming" (70). Whereas Schmitt's thrust in 1927 has an enemy in view by whom "the political is robbed, with special pathos, of all independence and is subordinated to the norms and 'orders' of morals and law" (I, 30), in 1932 Schmitt believes himself already able to look back at the "liberal age"[21] in which "political view-

20. Schmitt's reference to the October Revolution and the Revolution of 1789 should be mentioned as important exceptions that serve him as evidence that "everywhere in political history, in foreign policy as in domestic politics, the incapacity or unwillingness" to distinguish between friend and enemy appears "as a symptom of the political end." "In an exhausted Europe a relativist bourgeoisie makes the most exotic cultures imaginable into objects of its aesthetic consumption" (I, 26–27).

21. ". . . [T]hat production and consumption, profitability and market, have their own sphere and cannot be directed by ethics or aesthetics or religion is in all likelihood one of the few really valid, entirely unquestionable principles of today's world" (I, 30). "That production and consumption, setting of prices and market, have their own sphere and can be directed neither by ethics nor by aesthetics, nor by religion, and least of all by politics, was regarded as one of the few really indisputable, unquestionable dogmas of this liberal age" (71–72). Compare likewise the statement cited in n. 20 above with the new edition: "In a confused Europe a relativist bourgeoisie sought to make the most exotic cultures imaginable into objects of its aesthetic consumption" (67).

points were robbed, with special pathos, of all validity and subordinated to the normative prescriptions and 'orders' of morals, law, and economics" (72). Meanwhile, a mighty opponent to the "neutralizations and depoliticizations of important domains" has arisen in the "*total* state, which is not disinterested regarding any domain and potentially encompasses every domain." For this opponent "*everything* is, at least potentially, political" (24). In view of this situation Schmitt takes the offensive. Instead of reclaiming for the political its "own domain," he now aims at the whole. The "own, relatively independent, relatively ultimate distinctions" that the "political must have" (I, 3) are replaced by the "own, ultimate distinctions" of the political (26). The "point of the political" can be reached "from every 'domain'" (62); the political can "spring up" everywhere, penetrate and encompass everything, because it describes not a domain of its own, not a matter peculiar to it, but the "most extreme degree of intensity of a bond or a separation, of an association or a dissociation."[22] The conception of domains is replaced by a model of intensity. It is only consistent that Schmitt, seeking to the best of his ability to hide his far-reaching change, now says that the

22. 27, 38. "By the word 'political,' no domain of its own and no matter of its own is denoted that could be distinguished from other domains or matters, but only the *degree of intensity* of an association or dissociation. Every domain can become political if the object of a grouping into friends and enemies is derived from it. The word 'political' describes *not a new matter*, but . . . only a '*new turn*' . . . The achievement of a normal state consists in relativizing the opposed groupings within it and preventing the ultimate consequence thereof, war. If a state is no longer capable of that achievement, the center of gravity of politics shifts from foreign to domestic affairs. The oppositions within domestic politics then become the authoritative groupings into friends and enemies, and that plainly means latent or acute civil war." *Hugo Preuss. Sein Staatsbegriff und seine Stellung in der deutschen Staatslehre* (Tübingen, 1930), note 1, p. 26. Cf. "Staatsethik und pluralistischer Staat," *Positionen und Begriffe*, pp. 140–41, where the concept of intensity is oriented *entirely* toward the *political unit* in the form of the state; further, *Der Hüter der Verfassung* (Tübingen, 1931), p. 111.

distinction between friend and enemy can "exist theoretically and practically without *all those*[23] moral, aesthetic, economic, or other distinctions having to be applied at the same time" (27). *That* they come into play, individually or reinforcing one another, when the intensity of a bond or a separation rises to the "point of the political," can hardly be denied. The coming into play of these distinctions necessarily results as soon as the political itself is severed from all prior conditions, stripped of all substance, and taken to refer to "only the *degree of intensity* of an association or dissociation of men whose motives can have a religious, national (in the ethnic or cultural sense), economic, or other character" (38). The concept of the intensity of the political allows Schmitt to encompass civil war and revolution. Now the enemy can easily be conceived as the relative, the brother, the equal. Disregarding that consequence, Schmitt adheres to his statement that the enemy is "plainly the other, the alien." True, he does not neglect to make a subtle correction here too. In the first edition it is the political enemy who "in case of conflict signifies the negation of one's own kind of existence." In 1932, Schmitt says of each of the participants that "only he himself can decide whether the negation of his own kind of existence is signified in the otherness of the alien in the concrete, present case of conflict, and therefore whether that otherness will be fended off or fought in order to preserve one's own, proper kind of life."[24] However things may stand regarding this otherness of the enemy, which *qua otherness* is supposed to signify the negation of one's own kind of existence, the decision how to respond to this otherness cannot dispense with the categories good and evil,

23. My emphasis.
24. 27. Cf. ". . . must be fended off or fought in order to save one's own, proper kind of life" (III, 8).

noble and base, useful and harmful. How else are the viewpoints of "right knowing and understanding" (27) to be
gained, how else could one's own, proper kind of life, which
is to be preserved, be defined, articulated, delimited?
By turning away from the conception of domains,
Schmitt renders his concept of the political "capable of
encompassing civil war." The rise of the "total state"
makes one's vision keener for the "potential ubiquity" of
the political, and opens up the prospect of beating liberalism on its own turf, domestic politics. Schmitt's model of
intensity takes these developments into account.[25] It wid-

25. Schmitt attempted—not without success—to give the impression that
there were no conceptual changes at all in the *Concept of the Political*. He says in the
Afterword, dated "October 1931," to the second edition: "The present edition
contains . . . a series of new formulations, notes, and examples, but no alteration
or advance in the line of thought itself. Before making such changes I would
like to wait and see which directions and viewpoints will emerge as decisive in
the new discussion, which for about a year has been pursued vigorously, of the
political problem." For "about a year" Schmitt had begun, in initial, scattered
remarks, to operate with the model of intensity (cf. n. 22 above) and to diagnose
the "turning to the total state" (he published an essay with this title in April,
1931, in the *Europäische Revue*). In 1937, with a view to the conceptual pair *total
state–total war*, Schmitt says: "In Germany the development of the concept of
the political from 1927 onward expanded the connection of these totalities to the
series total enemy, total war, total state. Ernst Jünger's text *Totale Mobilmachung*
(1930) brought about the emergence of the formula into the general consciousness." "Totaler Feind, totaler Krieg, totaler Staat," *Positionen und Begriffe*, p.
235. In the *text* of 1927, though, none of the three named concepts occurs. In
1939, in a note on the republication of excerpts of the first edition of the *Concept
of the Political* in the collection *Positionen und Begriffe*, Schmitt says: "The present
reprint has followed literally the 1927 publication in order to make possible a
better evaluation of the attempts made by emigrant journals to represent as
indecent changes in my opinion a number of improvements that I made later"
(p. 314). If we disregard the fact that the criticism to which Schmitt alludes
referred to the changes made vis-à-vis not the first edition but the second (for
example, the two passages with the new formulations "suited to the time" that
Löwith adduces did not even occur in the text of 1927; see n. 6 above), it is of
interest in our context that in his reprint Schmitt includes only pages 11 (paragraph 13) to 21 (paragraph 23) but not pages 1–11 and 22–33 (paragraphs 1–12
and 24–33). The substantively most informative changes—the turning away from
the conception of domains, the withdrawal from the rhetoric of "pure
politics"—concern those very pages that Schmitt does not reprint.

ens the field of battle to the same degree that it gradualizes the political or makes it fluid. If "every concrete opposition is more political, the more it approaches the most extreme point, the grouping into friend and enemy" (30), then everything is *more* or *less*—and at all events potentially—political. On the other hand, the political can be conceived as the ubiquitously attainable degree of intensity only if the political is no longer bound to substantial oppositions grounded in nature or history, only if the political enemy does not remain limited to the "alien," to the "other" in a transindividual sense. "Pure politics" belongs to the past in 1932. Civil war is mentioned in the same breath as war.[26] Domestic politics appears side by side with foreign politics; Schmitt introduces an ancillary construction in order to provide the political *within* the state at least a limited space beyond the equating of politics and police, without the need for the political unity immediately to become engulfed in civil war: "*beside* the primary political decisions and under the protection of the decision that has been made," Schmitt declares, "numerous *secondary* concepts of 'political' arise" (30). But now he also comes to speak in detail of the "internal enemy," in the pithy meaning of the word, of the "intrastate declaration of enmity," of "dissenters and heretics" (46–48). Finally, war itself appears no longer as merely "armed conflict between nations." To Schmitt, the "holy wars and crusades" of the Church are now "actions that are based, like other wars, on a decision about the enemy" (48). In these actions, should not the enemy be dismissed "simultaneously in moral and other categories," as in those "especially intense and inhuman wars" that Schmitt, in 1932 too, characterizes as "going beyond the political"? Should it not be true of holy wars and cru-

26. 32, 33, 38, 46; cf. 29, 30–32, 42, 43, 47, 53, 54.

sades what is true of wars that make the enemy "into an
inhuman monster that must not only be fended off, but
definitively annihilated," that "thus" (here he departs from
the first edition) "is no longer only an enemy to be driven
back into his own boundaries"? With the concept of intensity, Schmitt leaves "pure politics" behind, but by no
means does he desire to forgo the advantages of his previous rhetoric. Thus he inserts into the text what can illumi-
nate his changed theoretical approach, without deleting
what can hardly accord with it but appears suited to make
a politically acceptable impression.[27] Thus he attempts to
maintain the fiction that "especially intense and inhuman
wars" could still in some compellingly significant sense be

---

27. In the reprint of the "unaltered" text, Schmitt italicizes the words "going
beyond the political," "annihilated," and "thus no longer only an enemy to be
driven back into his own boundaries" (37). In one of the "Remarks" of 1963 he
repeats the passage, calling it "decisive for the concept of the enemy that is
presupposed in the treatise" (119). The passage is so important to him that he also
cites it in full, verbatim (this time without italics), in the *Theorie des Partisanen.
Zwischenbemerkung zum Begriff des Politischen* (Berlin, 1963), p. 94. However things
may stand concerning the merits of Schmitt's later differentiation between the
"conventional," the "real," and the "absolute enemy" with regard to the theory
of war, that later differentiation is not decisive for the concept of the *political*. It
is in no way demanded, and certainly not given a foundation, by the concept of
the political. And the talk of the "especially intensive and inhuman wars" that,
going beyond the political, degrade the enemy, also gains no substance by means
of this distinction so long as the concept of intensity as constitutive of the political
is not itself abandoned. In the *Theorie des Partisanen*, two pages before he sets
forth the passage that still stems from the rhetoric of "pure politics" of 1927,
Schmitt writes: ". . . with those efforts to fence in war, European humanity
achieved something *rare:* renunciation of the criminalization of the opponent in
war, and thus the relativizing of enmity, the denial of absolute enmity. It is really
something *rare*, indeed *improbably* humane, to get men to renounce discrimina-
tion against and defamation of their enemies. That very renunciation now seems
to be put in question again by the guerrilla. After all, the *most extreme intensity of
political engagement* is one of his criteria. When Guevara says: 'The guerrilla is the
Jesuit of war,' he is thinking of the absoluteness of political commitment" (p.
92, my emphasis). Compare the statements of p. 93 with pp. 21, 88, 91, 94;
further, compare pp. 93–94 with the *Concept of the Political*, 67. On the use of
"going beyond the political," cf. also *Concept*, 55, 65, 66–67, 77–78.

called wars "that go beyond the political" when the political itself is supposed to denote the most extreme degree of intensity, a degree approached by oppositions between men ever more closely as these oppositions become more intense. No less misleading is the rhetoric of scholarly modesty to which Schmitt reverts in 1932 (26, 29). Schmitt's subject in the *Concept of the Political* is not merely or primarily the description of what is; nor does the political denote for him "only" a degree of intensity.[28] It is just as inadequate to say that the distinction between friend and enemy that he has in view represents or supplies a "simple criterion of the political."[29] How many conflicts escalate to military confrontations and therewith incontestably "refer to the real possibility of physical killing" without the participants' ever approaching the knowledge whether, or the decision that, "the otherness of the alien" "signifies the negation of one's own kind of existence"? It is wholly manifest that what Schmitt says about war applies equally to politics: according to the degree of enmity, politics can be more or less politics (III, 16). If politics, too, can be *more* or *less* political, if like "everything" else it is subject to the gradualization of the political, then the question arises, what kind of politics would Schmitt count as political "in the eminent sense," by what enmity do his statements about the "essence" of the political enemy take their bearings, what degree of intensity does he regard as the most extreme point of the political? Schmitt gives the answer in a new section of the 1932 edition, where he discusses the "peaks of great politics"; in that section the most profound

28. 38. In 1933 Schmitt deleted the word "only" (III, 21).

29. This statement (26), too, does not reappear in the third edition. (In 1927 Schmitt had spoken neither of the "simple criterion of the political" nor of the "criterion of the political" nor of the political's "own criteria." In 1932, these expressions occur six times altogether, pp. 23, 26, 27, 35.)

intention of the text is most strikingly expressed. "The peaks of great politics," he says there, "are at once the moments in which the enemy is discerned in concrete clarity as enemy" (67). They are the moments in which the enemy is *discerned*, in which he is *known* as the negation of one's own being, of one's own destiny—in which, and inseparably connected therewith, *one's own identity is established and gains a visible figure*.[TN3] When Schmitt immediately follows this statement with a historical example to illustrate what precisely appears to him to be a peak of *great politics*—an expression he uses nowhere else in the *Concept of the Political*[30]—he neither cites Machiavelli nor appeals to the authority of an expert in the *ius publicum Europaeum:* "For the modern age I see the most powerful outbreak of such an enmity . . . in Cromwell's battle against papal Spain." What is it that distinguishes that enmity from the "certainly not to be underestimated *écrasez l'infame* of the eighteenth century," what makes it "even stronger than Lenin's annihilating sentences against the bourgeois and Western capitalism"? In a speech of September 17, 1656, which Carl Schmitt uses as a medium for his self-explication, Cromwell declares the Spaniard the great enemy of the National Being; he defines him as a natural enemy "'by reason of that enmity that is in him against

30. In 1929, Schmitt said of Donoso Cortés that he has "the singular significance, in a time of relativizing dissolution of political concepts and oppositions and in an atmosphere of ideological fraud, of knowing the central concept of all great politics and of adhering to that concept through all deceptive and fraudulent obscurations and of seeking to get behind daily politics and define the great historical and essential distinction between friend and enemy." "Der unbekannte Donoso Cortés," in *Donoso Cortés in gesamteuropäischer Interpretation. Vier Aufsätze* (Cologne, 1950), p. 78. Compare, in light of the statement on the "image of the ultimate battle to the end between atheism and Christianity" (p. 75) and of the seemingly casual mention of the "genuine, always present and necessary eschatology" (p. 76), Schmitt's judgment on Donoso, pp. 7, 13, 15, 20, 21, 83, 105, 114. Cf. *Politische Theologie*, pp. 46, 51, 52, 54 (65, 73, 75, 79, 80).

whatsoever is of God. Whatsoever is of God which is in *you*, or which may be in you.' Then," Schmitt continues, "he repeats: The Spaniard is your enemy, his enmity is put into him by God; he is 'the natural enemy, the providential enemy'; he who considers him to be an accidental enemy does not know Scripture and the things of God, Who said, I will put enmity between thy seed and her seed (Gen. 3:15)." In the face of the providential enemy all further distinctions dissolve. He negates by the force of his being. The intensity of the opposition allows of no further increase.

III

Schmitt embarks upon his confrontation with liberalism in the name of the political, and he pursues it for the sake of religion. He defends the inescapable, and he fights for the inevitable. He confronts the "man who freely decides"—to whom everything essential appears to be a "private matter"—with a power by which man is entirely and existentially grasped; and he directs the man who needs security—to whom the verse applies, "He locks himself in and locks God out"—toward the present God Who tests him.[31] Schmitt's critique of liberalism thus flows into a critique that Leo Strauss, *en pleine connaissance de cause*, formulates as a critique of the "philosophy of culture": "one crux" of the "philosophy of culture" Strauss specifies as the "fact of religion"; the other he specifies as the "fact of the political."[32] Both religion and the fact of the political resist the parceling of human life into "autonomous provinces of culture"; both question "culture" as a "sovereign creation" or "pure product" of the human spirit; both subordinate human existence to the dominion, law, and command of an authority. Schmitt's increasing uneasiness and dissatisfaction with the modern concept of culture—which

31. "Zur Phonetik des Wortes Raum" (1942), in *Tymbos für Wilhelm Ahlmann. Ein Gedenkbuch* (Berlin, 1951), p. 243; *Donoso Cortés*, p. 114; cf. *Hugo Preuss*, p. 27.

32. Leo Strauss, *Philosophie und Gesetz. Beiträge zum Verständnis Maimunis und seiner Vorläufer* (Berlin, 1935), pp. 31 and 31n. Strauss expressly refers to the "Notes." He continues: "If 'religion' and 'politics' are *the* facts that transcend 'culture' or, to speak more exactly, are the *original* facts, then the radical critique of the concept of 'culture' is possible only in the form of a 'theological-political treatise,' which must, however, if it is not to lead again to the foundation of 'culture,' have the very opposite tendency to that of seventeenth-century theological-political treatises, especially those of Hobbes and Spinoza. To be sure, the first condition for such a treatise would be that these works of the seventeenth century no longer be understood, as has almost always happened so far, in the horizon of the philosophy of culture."

finds expression in 1930–31 in his disavowal of the conception of the political in terms of domains and can also be inferred from the changes in wording that he makes when republishing his 1929 speech "European Culture in the Intermediate Stages of Neutralization" in the *Concept of the Political*[33]—are grasped and articulated by Strauss in the most fundamental way imaginable. Not only does Strauss develop the "critique indicated by Schmitt of the prevailing concept of culture" (N10) inherent in the orientation toward the possibility of war as, simply, *the* dire emergency for man; not only does he reveal that critique as a determined attack on the doctrine of the "autonomy" of the various "domains of human thought and action." Strauss also takes a decisive step beyond the "indicated critique" and gives it a radical twist: against the prevailing concept of culture, according to which "not only the individual 'provinces of culture' in relation to one another" are autonomous, but, prior to them, culture as a whole is autonomous, Strauss raises the objection that that view "makes us forget that 'culture' always presupposes something that is cultivated: culture is always the *culture of nature*." Let culture be understood as the careful nurture of nature—"whether of the soil or of the human spirit

33. Schmitt deletes and replaces the words "culture" and "cultural" in the essay—the original title of which he leaves unmentioned in the Afterword (96)—no less than thirty-one times out of the original fifty-four occurrences. Ten times he deletes them without replacement, fifteen times he replaces them with "spiritual," once with "spirit," three times with "political," and twice with "politics." Two passages may be mentioned as examples: "All concepts of the [cultural] spiritual sphere, including the concept [culture] spirit, are in themselves pluralistic and can be understood only in terms of concrete [cultural] political existence" (84). "Technology is no longer a neutral ground in the sense of that process of neutralization, and every strong [culture] politics will make use of technology. Viewing the present century in a [cultural] spiritual sense as the technological century can therefore be only a provisional arrangement. The definitive meaning will arise only when it becomes clear which kind of [culture] politics is strong enough to gain control of the new technology" (94).

makes no difference"—or as a harsh and cunning fight against nature, "'culture' is certainly the culture of nature. 'Culture' is to such an extent the culture of nature that culture can be understood as a sovereign creation of the spirit only if the nature being cultivated has been presupposed to be the *opposite* of spirit, and been *forgotten*" (N10).

The twofold crux of the "philosophy of culture" does not induce Strauss to build on the answer of an authority, to prepare the path for such an answer, or to look for it himself. Instead, Strauss raises the question of nature. He asks about the human nature that precedes and underlies every culture. He poses the question of the *status naturalis*. In the course of his probing back into the hidden, disregarded, forgotten foundation of culture, Strauss has Schmitt bring the Hobbesian concept of the state of nature into a place of honor again: When Hobbes describes the *status naturalis* as the *status belli* simply, according to Strauss that description when translated into Schmitt's terminology means that the *status naturalis* is "the genuinely *political* status" (N11). Just as for Hobbes "the nature of war consisteth *not in actual fighting;* but in the known *disposition* thereto" (*Leviathan*, XIII), so for Schmitt the political lies "*not in fighting itself*" "but in a behavior that is determined by this real *possibility*" (37). The political, which Schmitt brings to bear as fundamental, is in Strauss's interpretation neither more nor less than the "state of nature" that the "philosophy of culture" has erased from memory. "Therewith the question about the genus within which the specific difference of the political is to be stipulated has also been answered: the political is a *status* of man; indeed, the political is *the* status as the 'natural,' the fundamental and extreme, status of man" (N11).

Strauss by no means fails to appreciate that Schmitt's

"state of nature" is defined "fundamentally differently" from that of Hobbes, that for Hobbes it is the "state of war of individuals," whereas for Schmitt it is the "state of war of groups (especially of nations)."[34] After going back to the supposedly common basis on which Schmitt and Hobbes meet one another, Strauss proceeds to accentuate, in contrast, the political opposition in which the two stand in relation to one another. Hobbes conceives the *status naturalis* as a state that is always necessarily oriented toward its own overcoming and negatively oriented toward the *status civilis*. With the polemical definition of the *bellum omnium contra omnes*, the abandonment of the "state of nature" is intended from the very beginning. "To this negation of the state of nature or of the political, Schmitt opposes the position of the political" (N12). The political opposition sought by Strauss in the two theoreticians' stance toward the state of nature—the Hobbesian negation and the Schmittian position of the political—is at first hidden by the fact that, according to Hobbes's teaching, the state of nature persists "at least" between nations and so there can be no question of Hobbes's "total negation" of the political. It therefore appears that Schmitt can adopt "Hobbes's polemic against the state of nature as the state of war of *individuals*" without having to question the political in the sense of the *Concept of the Political*, at least as long as the political is understood as "the 'natural' character of the relationships of human *groups*." But the difference becomes visible in its sharpest outline as soon as the political comes into view as the authoritative, as the dire emergency for the individual, as the existential claim by an authoritative power. According to Schmitt, the political unit can

34. "For Hobbes, in the state of nature everyone is the enemy of everyone else; for Schmitt, all political behavior is oriented toward *friend* and enemy" (N12).

demand of its members the readiness to die (46); according to Hobbes, the state—the end and limits of which are defined by an *individual's claim* based on natural right, a claim that is prior to the state—can justifiably demand only *conditional* obedience from the individual, "namely an obedience that does not stand in contradiction to the salvation or preservation of the life of this individual; for the securing of life is the ultimate basis of the state. Therefore, while man is otherwise obliged to unconditional obedience, he is under no obligation to risk his life; for death is the greatest evil" (N13). Strauss does not limit himself to making the opposition between Hobbes and Schmitt evident by the test of the dire emergency. He renders the opposition between the position and the negation of the political concrete by describing it as the conflict between the "position of the political" and the "position of civilization." He shows that the individualistic principles that cause Hobbes to negate the political in Schmitt's sense are the very same principles that, historically developed, finally underlie the project of the completely depoliticized and neutralized "unity of the world," against which Schmitt seeks to defend the "inescapability of the political." The principles that find expression in Hobbes's definition of the *salus populi*[35] "have to lead, as soon as 'humanity' becomes the subject or object of planning, to the ideal of civilization, that is, to the demand for rational social relations of humanity as *one* 'partnership in consumption and production' [58].

35. "Hobbes does not shrink from the consequence and expressly denies the status of courage as a virtue (*De homine* XIII 9). The same attitude is disclosed in his definition of the *salus populi*: the *salus populi* consists (1) in defense against the enemy from without; (2) in preservation of peace within; (3) in just and modest enrichment of the individual, which is much more readily attained through work and frugality than through victorious wars, and is particularly promoted by the nurture of mechanics and mathematics; (4) in the enjoyment of innocuous freedom (*De cive* XIII 6 and 14)" (N13).

Hobbes, to a much higher degree than Bacon, for example, is the author of the ideal of civilization. By this very fact, he is the founder of liberalism." Hobbes differs from developed liberalism "only, but certainly, by his knowing and seeing *against what* the liberal ideal of civilization has to be persistently fought for: not merely against rotten institutions, against the evil will of a ruling class, but against the natural evil of man; in an unliberal world Hobbes forges ahead to lay the foundation of liberalism against the—*sit venia verbo*—unliberal nature of man" (N13).

When Leo Strauss has Carl Schmitt (against the "philosophy of culture" as the "final self-awareness of liberalism," which, "sheltered by and engrossed in a world of culture," forgets human nature in its dangerousness and endangeredness) bestow new honor upon the Hobbesian concept of the "state of nature," Strauss consonantly has Schmitt return to Hobbes as the author of liberalism "in order to strike at the root of liberalism in Hobbes's express negation of the state of nature" (N14). Strauss's radical interpretation of what Schmitt not so much engages in as strives for contains this unspoken criticism: that the protagonist of the political achieves complete clarity neither about the position of the enemy nor about the presuppositions and requirements of his own project; and indeed, perhaps most surprisingly, that Schmitt did not recognize his most important theoretical antipode as an antipode at all. Strauss appends a footnote, the only footnote in the whole essay, to the statement that Schmitt returns, contrary to liberalism, to its author in order to strike at the root of liberalism in Hobbes; in that footnote he calls attention to the fact that Schmitt, in the first edition of the *Concept of the Political*, had described Hobbes as "by far the greatest and perhaps the sole truly systematic political thinker" (I, 25). Strauss continues: "Schmitt now speaks of Hobbes only as 'a great and truly systematic political thinker' [64]. In truth Hobbes is *the* antipolitical thinker ('political' understood in Schmitt's sense)." How does Schmitt respond to this challenge? He reacts in the same way as he reacts to Strauss's criticism of the incomplete break with the liberal "philosophy of culture's" thinking in terms of "domains" or "regions"—with deletions and insertions that take Strauss's "Notes" into account. In 1933, Hobbes has undergone metamorphosis from "by far the greatest and perhaps the sole truly systematic political thinker" via "a great and truly systematic political thinker" to "a great and truly systematic thinker," in whom, *"despite his extreme individualism,* the 'pessimistic' view of man *is so strong that it keeps the political understanding alive."* In an analogous way, the Hobbesian system of thought, which Schmitt in 1927 called *"his specifically political* system of thought" and, in 1932, appeared to Schmitt as at least *"a specifically political* system of thought," changes into "a system of thought that *still knows how to ask and answer specifically political questions."*[36] In each of the three substantive changes that Schmitt decides upon in the passage cited, he follows Strauss's line of argument: (1) Hobbes is not to be called a *political* thinker in Schmitt's sense; (2) Hobbes's individualistic principles, particularly his characterization of violent death as the greatest evil, conflict with the position of the political; (3) in contradistinction to developed liberalism, Hobbes knows and sees that the liberal project has to be persistently fought for against the unliberal nature of man. One can hardly say that Schmitt *answers* Strauss's arguments. He makes them, in this case, manifestly his own.

But Schmitt does not by any means let matters rest with

36. I, 25; 64–65; III, 46. My emphasis.

his spectacular reaction[37] concerning Thomas Hobbes. An initially inconspicuous change that occurs in a wholly different place proves just as illuminating and perhaps even more noteworthy since it was neither compelled nor occasioned by any direct criticism; first, however, the reader must understand the context in which the change draws its significance, a context established only by Strauss's interpretation. In order to elaborate the opposition in which Hobbes and Schmitt, rightly understood, stand in relation to one another, Strauss—while describing and explaining the "ideal of civilization" to which the Hobbesian principles ultimately lead—uses an expression that Schmitt employs to characterize the vision (his nightmare) of a fully depoliticized world. Strauss speaks of "rational social relations of humanity as *one* 'partnership in consumption and production,'" and he does not neglect to add the exact reference where Schmitt speaks of such a "partnership in consumption and production." In the third edition of the *Concept of the Political,* in the passage cited by Strauss, Schmitt changes "partnership in consumption and production" to *partnership in culture and consumption* (III, 40). In accordance with everything that Strauss develops and explains with a view to the "critique indicated by Schmitt of the prevailing concept of culture," Schmitt could hardly have expressed more pointedly and at the same time inconspicuously his agreement with the critique of the "philosophy of culture" in general as well as with the critique of its most significant forerunner in particular.[38] In the dia-

<hr>

37. Schmitt's reaction may be called spectacular not so much because of the attention that it has received as because of the clarity with which it proves that, and in what way, Schmitt in 1933 reacts to Strauss's "Notes."

38. In the Preface to the second edition of *Politische Theologie* (1934), Schmitt cautiously—and, in his text *Über die drei Arten des rechtswissenschaftlichen Denkens* (Hamburg, 1934), clearly—distances himself from Hobbes. Schmitt then provides what he had previously omitted, a political-theological critique of the

logue with Strauss, Schmitt's answer has all the greater
weight in that Strauss leaves no doubt, even in the details
of his formulations, that the existence for which the foundations are laid by Hobbes's principles is that very *existence
of the bourgeois* against which Schmitt seeks to maintain the
reality and necessity of the political. Strauss shows Schmitt
that the man of the Hobbesian system of thought is in fact
the bourgeois characterized by Schmitt (with recourse to
Hegel's "first polemical-political definition of the bourgeois") as a man "who does not want to leave the sphere
of the unpolitical, risk-free private, who in possession and
in the justice of private possession behaves as an individual
against the whole, who 'finds' the substitute for his political
nonentity in the fruits of peace and acquisition and, above
all, 'in the perfect *security* of the enjoyment of those things,'
who consequently wants to remain exempt from courage
and removed from the danger of a violent death."[39]

"founder of liberalism" to whom Strauss gives special attention in the "Notes,"
in the essay "Der Staat als Mechanismus bei Hobbes und Descartes" (*Archiv für
Rechts- und Sozialphilosophie*, vol. 30, no. 4 [1937], pp. 622–32) and in *Der Leviathan in der Staatslehre des Thomas Hobbes*.

39. 62. The emphasis of the word "security" derives from Schmitt and does
not occur in Hegel's text (*Wissenschaftliche Behandlungsarten des Naturrechts* [1802],
ed. Lasson, p. 383). Compare the statements by Strauss on Hobbes and the
"ideal of civilization" in the text and in n. 35 above with this definition of the
bourgeois. See also Leo Strauss, *Hobbes' politische Wissenschaft*, pp. 120 ff. —On
Schmitt's critique of the bourgeois cf. *Concept of the Political*, 35–36, 52, 58,
64, 67–68, 70, 93, 95; *Politische Theologie*, pp. 52, 54 (75–76, 78–79); *Römischer
Katholizismus und politische Form*, pp. 25, 42–43, 58–60 (17, 28, 38–39); *Politische
Romantik*, 2d ed. (Munich and Leipzig, 1925) (with an important new Preface
dated "September 1924," pp. 3–28), pp. 19, 20, 21, 26, 133, 141; *Die geistesgeschichtliche Lage des heutigen Parlamentarismus*, 2d ed. (Munich and Leipzig, 1926),
pp. 46, 58, 81, 86–87; *Verfassungslehre* (Munich and Leipzig, 1928), pp. 253, 256;
"Wesen und Werden des faschistischen Staates," in *Positionen und Begriffe*, pp.
110–11, 113, 114; *Staatsgefüge und Zusammenbruch des zweiten Reiches. Der Sieg des
Bürgers über den Soldaten* (Hamburg, 1934), p. 36; *Donoso Cortés*, p. 84.

IV

Schmitt's affirmation of the political, in Strauss's interpretation, is the affirmation of the "state of nature." The affirmation of the "state of nature" as the *status belli* simply is not intended to be bellicose, however, and thus does not signify the affirmation of war. Schmitt is concerned, rather, with the "relinquishment of the security of the status quo" (93). Security is to be relinquished "not because war would be something 'ideal,'" but because "it is necessary to return from the 'comfort and ease of the existing status quo' to the 'cultural or social nothing,' to the 'secret, humble beginning,' 'to the undamaged, noncorrupt nature' [93], so that 'out of the power of a pure and whole knowledge . . . the order of the human things' can arise again [95]" (N29). To Schmitt, the movement sketched by Strauss of returning to unaltered nature is essentially a movement of departure, of opposition, of negation. Schmitt's affirmation of the political receives its concrete form from the rejection of the existence of the bourgeois. The polemical meaning of that affirmation lies in the negation of the "ideal of civilization," whose advocates, claiming to usher in a society without politics and without state, want to elevate—or must elevate—bourgeois existence to the universal destiny of everything that has a human face.

According to Strauss, Schmitt "ultimately by no means repudiates as utopian" the ideal of a globe that has been definitively pacified and depoliticized "—he says, after all, that he does not know whether it cannot be realized—but he does abhor it. That Schmitt does not display his views in a moralizing fashion but endeavors to conceal them only makes his polemic the more effective. Let us listen to Schmitt himself!: 'if . . . the distinction between friend and enemy ceases even as a mere possibility, there will

only be a politics-free weltanschauung, culture, civilization, economy, morals, law, art, *entertainment,* etc., but
there will be neither politics nor state' [54]. We have emphasized the word 'entertainment' because Schmitt does
everything to make entertainment *nearly* disappear in a series of man's serious pursuits; above all, the 'etc.' that immediately follows 'entertainment' glosses over the fact that
'entertainment' is really the ultimate term in the series, its
finis ultimus. Schmitt thus makes it clear: . . . politics and
the state are the only *guarantee* against the world's becoming a world of entertainment; therefore, what the opponents of the political want is ultimately tantamount to the
establishment of a world of entertainment, a world of
amusement, a world without *seriousness*" (N27). According
to Schmitt, in a "world without the distinction between
friend and enemy and consequently a world without politics" there could "be various, perhaps very interesting, oppositions and contrasts, competitions and intrigues of all
kinds, but no opposition on the basis of which it could
sensibly be demanded of men that they sacrifice their
lives" (35–36). Even this polemical description of the apolitical counterproject (a description in which the central
statement only repeats tautologically what is stated in
Schmitt's very concept of the political) achieves its goal and
unfolds its meaning precisely by what Schmitt expresses
indirectly: In a world without politics there is nothing, but
in a political world there may very well be something, for
which the sacrifice of a life could *sensibly* be demanded.
"Here, too, what Schmitt concedes to the pacifists' ideal
state of affairs, what he *finds striking* about it, is its capacity
to be interesting and entertaining; here, too, he takes pains
to hide the criticism contained in the observation '*perhaps
very interesting.*' He does not, of course, wish to call into
doubt whether the world without politics is interesting: if

he is convinced of anything, it is that the apolitical world is *very* interesting ('competitions and intrigues of all sorts'); the 'perhaps' only questions, but certainly *does* question, whether this capacity to be interesting can claim the interest of a human being worthy of the name; the 'perhaps' conceals and betrays Schmitt's *nausea* over this capacity to be interesting, which is only possible if man has forgotten what genuinely matters" (N27).

Leo Strauss knows himself to be in agreement with Carl Schmitt in disapproving of a world-state, in rejecting the illusory security of a status quo of comfort and of ease, in holding in low esteem a world of mere entertainment and the mere capacity to be interesting. In no way does he fall shy of Schmitt in opposing an ideal that, should it ever be realized, would threaten to reduce humanity to a partnership for culture and consumption. He shares Schmitt's criticism of the "process of neutralization and depoliticization" in which modern Europe—in its search for "an absolutely and definitively neutral ground" (89) so as to avoid the quarrel over the right faith—has finally arrived at the faith in technology. He subscribes to Schmitt's objection to that striving for agreement and peace at all costs and to the resulting process which, in *Das Zeitalter der Neutralisierungen und Entpolitisierungen* (The Age of Neutralizations and Depoliticizations) is diagnosed as a protracted quarrel that occurs in flight from quarrel; or to put it more precisely, he formulates this objection himself with a clarity and keenness that discloses the pith of his confrontation with Schmitt: "Agreement at all costs is possible only as agreement at the cost of the meaning of human life; for agreement at all costs is possible only if man has relinquished asking the question of what is right; and if man relinquishes that question, he relinquishes being a man. But if he seriously asks the question of what is right, the quarrel will be ignited (in view of 'the inextricable set of problems' [90] this question entails), the life-and-death quarrel: the political—the grouping of humanity into friends and enemies—owes its legitimation to the seriousness of the question of what is right" (N28). The greatest proximity to Schmitt as well as the deepest difference from him are both contained in this critique, for Strauss bases the objection to neutralization and depoliticization not on the answer of political theology but on the question of political philosophy; he raises his objection in the name and for the sake of the question of what is right, of the right life, of the one thing needful. In so doing, however, Strauss places the critique that allies him with Schmitt, the critique of the exclusion of what is most important, onto a ground that is not at all Schmitt's ground. When Strauss characterizes the seriousness of the *question* of what is right as the *legitimation* of the political, what is meant is first that the question of what is right *has to be asked;* and what is further implied is that basically, in the *most fundamental* respect, that question can be answered by means of human reason. Schmitt, however, believes that the one thing needful can only be believed in because it *is* faith; that the question on which everything ultimately depends is not a question *asked by man* but the question *put to man,* whether he will obey God or Satan; and that the political finds its ultimate foundation in the inevitability of this question. Schmitt knows why he has the "sequence of stages" of the neutralizations and depoliticizations begin with the "step taken by the seventeenth century in moving from the received Christian theology to the system of a 'natural' scientific approach" (88); and there is a greater logical rigor than the immediate context of his historical construction might make apparent in Schmitt's recognition (from the viewpoint of his political theology) of that step, which for him describes the turning away from faith in particular Providence as "the strongest and most consequential of all intellectual turns in European history."[40] *Inter auctoritatem et philosophiam nihil est medium.* The gulf between political theology and political philosophy is insuperable,[41] dividing Carl Schmitt and Leo Strauss even where both seem to agree in their political positions or in fact agree in their political critique of a common opponent.

For all the agreement and confirmation, this gulf finds expression, discreetly but quite clearly, in Schmitt's direct

40. "I regard this step as the strongest of all cultural turns in European history" (wording of the first edition of 1929, p. 524). Regarding the "consequences": "The concepts that were developed in many centuries of theological thought are now becoming uninteresting and are turning into a private matter. God Himself is evicted from the world in the metaphysics of deism in the eighteenth century and becomes a neutral arbiter vis-à-vis the battles and oppositions of real life; as Hamann said against Kant, He becomes a concept and ceases to be a being" (89). On the turning away from faith in particular Providence, see also *Politische Theologie*, pp. 37, 44 (49, 62), and *Politische Romantik*, p. 137. Cf. *Der Leviathan in der Staatslehre des Thomas Hobbes*, pp. 64–70, 79, 82–83, 85–86; note especially p. 87. Precisely because in his book on the Leviathan Schmitt acknowledges Hobbes's key role in the "decisive first step" on the path to "the neutralization of every truth, a neutralization that culminates in technologizing"—the literally central sentence of the book reads: "But the idea of the state as a technologically perfected *magnum artificum* created by man, as a machine that has its 'right' and its 'truth' only in itself, that is, in performance and in function, was first grasped and systematically developed as a clear concept by Hobbes" (p. 70)—it is of great importance to him that Hobbes "remained in the Christian faith," that for Hobbes "Jesus was the Christ," and that out of "genuine piety" Hobbes attempted to give an answer to the challenge of his concrete situation (p. 126; cf. pp. 20–21 and 71–72; "Die vollendete Reformation. Bemerkungen und Hinweise zu neuen Leviathan-Interpretationen," in *Der Staat*, vol. 4, no. 1 (1965), pp. 62–63 and 58n.).

41. Cf. Leo Strauss, *What Is Political Philosophy?* (Glencoe, IL, 1959), p. 13; *The City and Man* (Chicago, 1964), p. 241; *Die Religionskritik Spinozas als Grundlage seiner Bibelwissenschaft. Untersuchungen zu Spinozas Theologisch-politischem Traktat* (Berlin, 1930), pp. 183, 222; "Jerusalem and Athens. Some Preliminary Reflections" (1967), in *Studies in Platonic Political Philosophy* (Chicago, 1983), pp. 149–51, 155, 157, 162, 166, 170, 171–72; "The Mutual Influence of Theology and Philosophy" (1954), in *The Independent Journal of Philosophy*, vol. 3 (1979), pp. 112, 113, 114; *On Tyranny*, rev. ed. (New York, 1963), pp. 109, 210; *The Argument and the Action of Plato's Laws* (Chicago, 1975), pp. 29, 59.

response to the exegesis of his polemic against the utopia of a definitively pacified globe. Schmitt's agreement can be inferred from his retaining unaltered in the thoroughly revised text the formulations that Strauss had emphasized and used as a basis for his detailed interpretation. In 1933, too, Schmitt speaks of the "perhaps very interesting oppositions and contrasts," of the "competitions and intrigues of all kinds" that "could exist" in a world without politics (III, 18); the "series of serious pursuits" that remain in such a state of affairs, the series in which he *nearly* makes entertainment disappear by using an "etc." to glass over the fact that entertainment "is really the ultimate term in the series, its *finis ultimus*," likewise recurs word for word. Schmitt's agreement does not remain tacit, however. With a telling addendum, he expands the core statement to which Strauss had directed the reader's attention: ". . . were . . . the distinction between friend and enemy *wholly* to cease even as a mere possibility," Schmitt says in the third edition, "*men would thus have achieved the full security of their this-worldly enjoyment in life. The old tenet that man is not to expect full security in this life*—plena securitas in hac vita non expectanda—*would be obsolete*. There *would consequently also be* neither politics nor state, but only a politics-free weltanschauung, culture, civilization, economy, morals, law, art, entertainment, etc."[42] With this insertion, Schmitt

---

42. III, 36. My emphasis. In one of the "Remarks" of 1963 regarding the text of 1932, Schmitt writes: "In his discussion of 1932 . . . on page 745 Leo Strauß puts his finger on the word 'entertainment.' He is right to do so. The word is altogether inadequate here and corresponds to the (at that time) incomplete state of the reflection. Today I would say 'play' [*Spiel*] to express more pithily the conceptual opposition (which Leo Strauß rightly discerned) to 'seriousness' . . . In all these statements '*Spiel*' should be translated as 'play' and would still leave open a kind of enmity, albeit conventional, between the 'opponents.' Things are different in the mathematical theory of the 'game' [*Spiel*] . . . In my makeshift word 'entertainment,' however, there are also concealed references to sports, leisure activity, and the new phenomena of an 'affluent society,' and I had not

emphatically corroborates Strauss's interpretation. Schmitt incorporates it in a certain way into his own presentation. He is using it to clarify the thrust of his criticism when, in this very passage, he makes a detour to the Hegelian definition cited elsewhere (III, 43–44) of the bourgeois: A world without politics would be, as Strauss rightly emphasizes, a world of entertainment, of amusement, a world without seriousness.[43] It would be a world that can be named with a polemically-politically defined, historical and concrete name. It would be the world of the bourgeois raised to universality, expanded to the point of excluding everything else—the world of the bourgeois who finds his satisfaction in the perfect security of the enjoyment of the

---

become sufficiently conscious of these developments in the then still prevalent climate of the German philosophy of work" (120–21). One may be permitted to doubt that this "Remark" appropriately represents, to say nothing of attaining, the level of the reflection of 1932. If "play" is to leave "open a conventional kind of enmity," the statement in the text (54) to which Schmitt refers becomes nonsensical, because there Schmitt wants to characterize the state of affairs in which the "distinction between friend and enemy ceases even as a mere possibility." Thus *if* the word "play" *did have* the "advantage" over "entertainment" of not excluding a conventional enmity, which per definitionem "must have and maintain reference to the real possibility of physical killing" (33; cf. *Theorie des Partisanen*, pp. 17, 56, 76, 90, 92), then "play," for that very reason, would not be a suitable "replacement" for "entertainment." But as for "the references to sports, leisure activity, and the new phenomena of an 'affluent society,'" precisely these make "entertainment" the proper word to express what Schmitt in 1932 *wanted* to express and what—*after* Strauss had put his finger on the formulation, which was anything but "inadequate"—he clearly expressed beyond any doubt in 1933.

43. "En fait, la fin du Temps humain ou de l'Histoire, c'est-à-dire l'anéantissement définitif de l'Homme proprement dit ou de l'Individu libre et historique, signifie tout simplement la cessation de l'Action au sens fort du terme. Ce qui veut dire pratiquement:—la disparition des guerres et des révolutions sanglantes. Et encore la disparition de la *Philosophie;* car l'Homme ne changeant plus essentiellement lui-même, il n'y a plus de raison de changer les principes (vrais) qui sont à la base de sa connaisance du Monde et de soi. Mais tout le reste peut se maintenir indéfiniment; l'art, l'amour, le jeu, etc., etc.; bref, tout ce qui rend l'Homme *heureux.*"[TN4] Alexandre Kojève, *Introduction à la lecture de Hegel* (Paris, 1947), p. 435n. Cf. also "Note de la Seconde Edition," pp. 436–37.

fruits of peace and of acquisition. Abhorrence and nausea over such a world, in which no room remains for a "demanding moral decision,"[44] induce Schmitt to defend the political. Abhorrence and nausea stand in the background of his affirmation of the "state of nature," and it is by means of that affirmation that the "security of the status quo"—the security in which the existence of the bourgeois is absorbed—is to be relinquished. Thus Strauss's distillation is confirmed. Schmitt "affirms the political because he sees in the threatened status of the political a threat to the seriousness of human life. The affirmation of the political is ultimately nothing other than the affirmation of the moral" (N27). Now, however, Schmitt in his answer to Strauss speaks expressly of the security of *this-worldly* enjoyment of life and of the tenet that man is not to expect full security in *this* life. Schmitt takes care, moreover, to repeat in Latin the "old tenet" that advances this teaching. Furthermore, he transposes the whole statement from the indicative to the hypothetical subjunctive. And, finally, he changes the statement itself, its structure, the meshing of the argument: *If the distinction between friend and enemy ceases, there will be neither politics nor state* is replaced with: *were* the distinction between friend and enemy *wholly to cease, men would have reached the full security of their this-worldly enjoyment of life;* the Augustinian maxim "plena securitas in hac vita non expectanda" *would be obsolete; consequently* there would *also* be neither politics nor state. In everything—in his choice of words, his reference to Augustine, the change of verbal mood, the restructuring of the argument—Schmitt intimates what he is building on when he affirms the political, what he is certain of when he denies the security of

44. *Politische Theologie*, p. 56 (83). Cf. *Politische Romantik*, pp. 21, 25, 96–97, 222; *Die geistesgeschichtliche Lage*, pp. 68–69, 77, 80, 81, 83.

the man who needs security. The distinction between friend and enemy could "entirely cease even as a mere possibility" only if Genesis 3:15 had no validity, only if there were no Providential enemy, only if men lived in a paradisiacal secular world and did not have to face the decision between good and evil or to "answer" for their choices. Ultimately, for Schmitt the affirmation of the political is nothing but the affirmation of the moral. But Schmitt sees the affirmation of the moral as itself based in the theological.[45] For him the affirmation of the moral is part of his political theology.

When Leo Strauss disparages a world that is merely entertaining and interesting, he does so because the men in that world remain far beneath the potential of their nature and are capable of actualizing neither their most noble nor their most excellent faculties. He rejects the illusory security of a status quo of comfort and ease because a life that does not subject itself to the danger of radical questioning and the exertion of self-examination appears to him to be not worth living. A comfortable, cosy interior hinders liberation from the cave and ascent into the open. Strauss rejects the homogeneous world-state because he recognizes it as the state of Nietzsche's "last man" and because he sees the end of the particular political community as followed by the end of philosophy on earth.[46] Schmitt opposes the "world-state" because he perceives it as an antigodly attempt to construct paradise on earth. To him, the striving for "Babylonian unity" is the expression of man's making himself into a god. The "religion of technicity" (93, 94), the "faith in man's unlimited power and dominion over

45. Cf. Leo Strauss, *Persecution and the Art of Writing* (Glencoe, IL, 1952), p. 140.

46. Leo Strauss, *De la tyrannie*, pp. 295, 310–11, 342–44; *On Tyranny*, pp. 211–15, 223, 226; *The City and Man*, pp. 4–6.

nature, indeed over human *physis*, in the unlimited 'shrinking of natural limits,' in the unlimited potential for change
and for happiness in the natural this-worldly existence of
man" (93), would reach its culmination in the "world-
state." The process of neutralization and depoliticization
would come to its conclusion in a "business" of global
extent, in which it appears that "things administer themselves" but in fact the *Antichrist* has begun to establish his
dominion.[47] In 1916, Schmitt for the first time described
the horror associated, in his view, with that dominion. The
reason for the horror is that the Antichrist "knows how to
imitate Christ and to make himself so similar to Him that
he swindles all men out of their souls." "His mysterious
power lies in the imitation of God. God created the world;
the Antichrist counterfeits it . . . The sinister magician
recreates the world, changes the face of the earth, and
subdues nature. Nature serves him; for what purpose is a
matter of indifference—for any satisfaction of artificial
needs, for ease and comfort. Men who allow themselves
to be deceived by him see only the fabulous effect; nature
seems to be overcome, the age of security dawns; everything has been taken care of, a clever foresight and planning replace Providence; the Antichrist 'makes' Providence
as he makes any institution."[48] The Antichrist would tri-

47. *Politische Theologie*, pp. 44, 45, 56 (62, 65, 82); *Römischer Katholizismus*, pp.
31–32, 56 (21, 37); *Politische Romantik*, p. 21; "Staatsethik und pluralistischer
Staat," in *Positionen und Begriffe*, p. 143; "Nachwort" to *Disputation über den
Rechtsstaat* (Hamburg, 1935), p. 87; "Die Lage der europäischen Rechtswissenschaft" (1943–44), in *Verfassungsrechtliche Aufsätze aus den Jahren 1924–1954*
(Berlin, 1958), p. 426; *Donoso Cortés*, pp. 11, 91, 108, 110–11, 112; "Die Einheit
der Welt," in *Merkur*, vol. 6, no. 1 (January 1952), pp. 1–2, 8–9, 10; "Nomos-
Nahme-Name," p. 102; *Theorie des Partisanen*, pp. 62, 73–74, 79; *Politische Theologie II. Die Legende von der Erledigung jeder Politischen Theologie* (Berlin, 1970), pp.
46 and 124–26.
48. *Theodor Däublers "Nordlicht." Drei Studien über die Elemente, den Geist und
die Aktualität des Werkes* (Munich, 1916), pp. 65–66; cf. 63.

umph—and in the long run could *only* triumph—if he succeeded in convincing men that the opposition between friend and enemy has been overcome once and for all, that they no longer need to decide between Christ and Antichrist. In describing the ideal of a definitively pacified globe, a world without politics, life without seriousness, Schmitt is fighting the "empire of the Antichrist." In affirming the political, by his own self-understanding he affirms not the state of nature but an eschatologically conceived *state of historicity*, a state of *demanding moral decision*, or *probation* and *judgment*.[49] And, like every Christian theoretician who "gives the writings of Moses the credence he owes them," Schmitt denies that men ever existed or could exist in a state of nature.[50]

49. "Die Sichtbarkeit der Kirche," pp. 75–76, 78; *Politische Theologie*, pp. 50, 55, 56 (71, 80, 82, 83); *Römischer Katholizismus*, pp. 31–32, 39–40, 65–66, 79–80 (21, 26, 43, 52); *Politische Romantik*, pp. 21, 25, 104; *Der Nomos der Erde im Völkerrecht des Jus Publicum Europaeum* (Cologne, 1950), pp. 33, 75–77, 102; "Nomos-Nahme-Name," pp. 104–5; *Donoso Cortés*, pp. 76, 78, 114; *Ex Captivitate Salus. Erfahrungen der Zeit 1945–47* (Cologne, 1950), pp. 31, 52, 58, 61, 68, 75, 78; "Die geschichtliche Struktur des heutigen Welt-Gegensatzes von Ost und West," in *Freundschaftliche Begegnungen. Festschrift für Ernst Jünger zum 60. Geburtstag* (Frankfurt/Main, 1955), pp. 149–52; *Politische Theologie II*, pp. 72, 75; and "Drei Möglichkeiten eines christlichen Geschichtsbildes," in *Universitas*, vol. 5, no. 8 (1950), pp. 927–31. (The essay appeared with the unauthorized title "Drei Stufen historischer Sinngebung." By hand, Schmitt restored the original title in reprints that he sent out. He says that the "title improvised by the editors" is "wholly wrong; neither 'stages' nor 'attribution of meaning' is involved.")

50. Cf. Jean-Jacques Rousseau, *Discours sur l'origine et les fondemens de l'inégalité parmi les hommes*. Kritische Edition (Paderborn, 1984), *Exordium*, p. 70.

V

Strauss pursues his confrontation with Schmitt on the plane of political philosophy. He interprets the *Concept of the Political* as though he were interpreting the text of a theoretician who merely lays claim to a knowledge that is accessible to man as man, or as though only such a knowledge were of significance for the confrontation he is pursuing. In this way he makes Schmitt's position as strong as it can possibly be made if the political theology on which it rests is abstracted from it. With the questions raised by Strauss's interpretation, with the *aporiai* that it points out in Schmitt's conception, Strauss induces Schmitt to give answers that make the background of faith, which is omitted by Strauss, emerge all the more clearly. Strauss's challenge has the effect that in 1933 the author of the *Concept of the Political* discloses more of his identity as a political theologian than he had revealed in 1927 or 1932.

The thrust of the Straussian interpretation finds especially striking expression in the discussion of what support Schmitt enlists to demonstrate that the political is the inescapable. Can he even demonstrate it? According to Schmitt's express statement, "all genuine political theories" presuppose man to be "'evil,' that is, to be not at all an unproblematic but a 'dangerous' and dynamic being" (61). The position of the political thus seems to have its "ultimate presupposition" in man's dangerousness, even though, as Strauss hastens to add, this train of thought "is in all probability not Schmitt's last word" and "certainly not the most profound thing that he has to say" (N20). If the political stands or falls on the dangerousness of man, everything depends on knowing whether his dangerousness is unshakable, his evil inescapable: "the necessity of the political is as certain as man's dangerousness" (N21).

Now Strauss indicates that Schmitt himself qualifies the thesis of dangerousness as a *"supposition,"* as an "anthropological confession of *faith*" (58). "But if man's dangerousness is *only supposed or believed in, not genuinely known*,[51] the opposite, too, can be regarded as possible, and the attempt to eliminate man's dangerousness (which until now has always really existed) can be put into practice. If man's dangerousness is *only believed in*,[52] it is in principle *threatened*, and therewith the political is threatened also" (A21). The inescapability of the political amounts to nothing so long as one tries to base it on the foundations on which Schmitt erects the theoretical edifice of his concept of the political. They hold no weight. They do not bear up under criticism. The abstraction from Schmitt's political theology escalates here into a barely concealed attack: the substantive rejection could hardly be keener. For of course it did not remain concealed from Strauss that for Schmitt the "thesis of dangerousness" has by no means the status of a mere supposition, nor did it escape him that Schmitt's talk of an "anthropological confession of faith" sets the tone for a chapter in which the real intention consists in anchoring the political in the theological. Precisely for that reason Strauss opposes knowledge to faith, and for the same reason he categorically emphasizes that faith does not suffice. In the center of the seventh chapter (devoted to "anthropology") of the *Concept of the Political*, Schmitt attempts to demonstrate that politics is founded on theology or, to choose a formulation that more appropriately expresses his strategy, to induce the reader to believe in such a foundational relationship. According to Schmitt, "the connection between political theories and theological dogmas of sin, a connection that

51. My emphasis.
52. My emphasis.

is especially striking in the works of Bossuet, Maistre, Bonald, Donoso Cortés, and F. J. Stahl[53] but influences just as intensely the writings of countless others," can be explained "in terms of the kinship" of the "necessary intellectual presuppositions" of theology and politics. "The basic theological dogma of the sinfulness of the world and of men, . . . just like the distinction between friend and enemy, leads to a division of men, to a 'distancing', and makes the indiscriminate optimism of a universal concept of man impossible. In a good world among good men, only peace, security, and harmony of all with all prevail naturally; here priests and theologians are just as superfluous as politicians and statesmen. Troeltsch (in his *Soziallehren der christlichen Kirchen* [Social Doctrines of the Christian Churches]) and Seillière (in many publications about romanticism and romantics) have shown by the example of numerous sects, heretics, romantics, and anarchists what the denial of original sin means for social and individual psychology. The methodological connection between theological and political intellectual presuppositions is thus clear" (64). Is it clear? Is the "kinship" of the "necessary intellectual presuppositions" merely a matter of a structural analogy, or does it express a common origin and point to one and the same foundation? Are we supposed to take the view of the "sociology of knowledge" and to see here merely a "parallel" that emerges from observation of the "spheres" of the theological and the political—a "distinction" and a "distancing," albeit of very different kinds, in each case—whereas, in turn, other "parallels" that allow of divergent classifications occur in, and to, other "domains of human thought"? Is the "jurist" who moves "in the

---

53. In 1933 Schmitt deleted the name Stahl (III, 45). Cf. III, 44, and *Der Leviathan in der Staatslehre des Thomas Hobbes*, pp. 106–10; see nn. 5 and 6 above.

region of research in the history of law and in sociology,"[54] speaking once again? Is Schmitt concerned with "explaining" why political theologians of the likes of Maistre, Bonald, or Donoso got trapped into building their political doctrines upon a theological dogma without being fully clear about what they were doing and why they were doing it? At the beginning of the chapter, Schmitt lets the reader know that "all theories of the state and all political ideas" could be divided according to whether they "presuppose a man 'by nature evil' or 'by nature good'" (59). There are thus political theories that exist in harmony with their "necessary intellectual presupposition" and others that do not. The theories that are in harmony with themselves are those that are in harmony with the basic dogma of sinfulness. Schmitt can recognize only them as "genuine political theories" (61). They alone are capable, in the best case, of doing justice to the reality of the political, because the political has its deepest foundation in original sin.

In 1933, the previous presentation of the connection between theology and politics does not appear sufficiently clear to Schmitt as neither to need nor to allow of clarification. Clarification is needed even regarding the heart of his anthropological confession of faith, namely original sin—an expression never once uttered by Strauss. Judging "what the denial of original sin means" is no longer to be left to the uncertain interpretation of the reader of Troeltsch and Seillière. It is proclaimed apodictically. E. Troeltsch and the Baron Seillière "have shown by the example of numerous sects, heretics, romantics, and anarchists that the denial of original sin destroys all social order" (III, 45). This statement tolerates no contradiction. Credo or non-credo,

---

54. *Politische Theologie II*, p. 101. Cf. on the same page Schmitt's rendering of the subtitle of the *Political Theology* of 1922; see pp. 22, 30, 98, 110.

order or disorder. The political theologian dares to press ahead, up to an Either/Or that demands a decision: for faith or for chaos. When Schmitt, as in 1927 and 1932, continues with the observation that "the methodological connection between theological and political intellectual presuppositions" is "thus clear," the dependency of the political (to begin with what is most obvious) in the relationship that exists for Schmitt between theology and politics is indeed sufficiently discernable. Politics needs theology. Without a seam, Schmitt picks up the thread of what he had already emphasized, with a view to the "deepest connections," in his *Political Theology* of 1922: "if the theological disappears, so does the moral; and if the moral disappears, so does the political idea."[55] The theological is the *conditio sine qua non*. Can the theological ever "disappear"? It may be denied. But if so, it is far from "having disappeared" or "having been disposed of." By replacing a single word in the sentence immediately preceding the statement about original sin, Schmitt gives a sign of just how little he believes in the possible disappearance of the theological and of the political and of how much he believes in the inescapability of both: "In a good world, among good men, only peace, security, and harmony of all with all prevail naturally; here the priests and theologians are just as *disturbing*[56] as the politicians and statesmen." Theologians and politicians will never be *superfluous*. Their existence does not, on its own, become unnecessary. They would have to be excluded, fought, eliminated. A world of peace and security would be established once and for all only if faith in the ultimate "distinction and division of men," the distinction "be-

---

55. *Politische Theologie*, p. 55 (82).
56. My emphasis.

tween the redeemed and the unredeemed, the chosen and the unchosen" (III, 45), were conquered and hence also the last possible source of "disturbance" exhausted.[57] In the end, politics needs theology not to realize a goal but to provide a foundation for its own necessity. Faith is the impregnable bastion of the political. The first of the three substantively relevant changes that Schmitt makes in the textual passage we are discussing refers emphatically to the same view of the "deepest connections." The connection between political theories and theological dogmas of sin "is explained" in the new edition of 1933 *"first in terms of the ontological-existential mentality that conforms to the essence of a theological, as well as a political, line of thought. But then* [the connection is explained] *also* in terms of the kinship of these methodological intellectual presuppositions."[58] In each case Schmitt is ultimately concerned not with instances of kinship, with parallels, or with analogies of structure, but solely with what constitutes the agreements between theology and politics. The "ontological-existential mentality" accords with the essence of a theological as well as a political line of thought because the "essence of the political" (20, 45) is equipped with a theological foundation, because the political by its essence has a theological destination. The inescapability of the distinction between friend and enemy in the political "sphere" "corresponds"

57. "Ipsi enim diligenter scitis, quia dies Domini sicut fur in nocte ita veniet. Cum enim dixerint: Pax et securitas! tunc repentinus eis superveniet interitus, sicut dolor in utero habenti, et non effugient." First Letter to the Thessalonians, 5:2–3. *"Pax et securitas"* is the slogan of the Antichrist in the famous *Ludus de Antichristo* (v. 414). Only in the passage of the First Letter to the Thessalonians cited are *pax* and *securitas* named in one breath in the Bible. "For when they shall say 'peace and security!' then sudden destruction cometh upon them." Cf. the Second Letter to the Thessalonians, 2. On *Ludus de Antichristo,* see *Politische Theologie II,* p. 61.
58. III, 45. My emphasis.

to the inevitability of the decision between God and Satan in the theological "sphere." Politics, like theology, claims to grasp man "wholly and existentially" (III, 21). If politics is destiny for a "political line of thought," religion is no less destiny for a theological line of thought. If "for political decisions even the mere possibility of right knowing and understanding, and therewith the entitlement to participate in discussion and to make judgments, is based only on the existential *sharing* and participating, only on the genuine *participatio*" (III, 8), such a basis applies nowhere more emphatically than in the case of the community of believers that leads itself back to the truth of the revelation in which it shares and that sees itself inseparably bound to existential participation in the One Truth, in the perfected *participatio*. The agreements between the two "spheres" lose the character of mere "correspondences," and the deepest connection between the theological and the political becomes visible in the light of the "only case that matters," the case from which and toward which Carl Schmitt's thought moves. The only case that matters is the battle with the Providential enemy, the enemy who is determined "historically and concretely" in the moments of great politics, and against whom finally, at the end of time, the "battle of decision" must be fought.

For the same reason for which man's dangerousness is unshakable to Schmitt, he does not conceive man's evil as *innocent* evil. Schmitt does not see himself as facing the task of nullifying the "view of human evil as animal and thus innocent 'evil'" (Strauss formulates this task with a view to "the radical critique of liberalism that Schmitt strives for" [N26]), because he does not subscribe to such a view. Schmitt also reveals this stance through his references to the theological foundation of his "anthropology."

If, as Strauss states,[59] the philosopher Hobbes had to understand natural evil "as *innocent* 'evil,'" because he denied sin" (N26), the same observation does not apply to Schmitt in any way. Original sin is the central point around which everything turns in his anthropological *confession* of faith. Schmitt has several reasons for expressly bringing into play the distinction between a man "by nature evil" and a man "by nature good" as a "wholly summary" distinction "not to be taken in a specifically moral or ethical sense"; for insisting "only" on a "problematical view of man" as the "precondition to all further political discussion" (59); and for considering it sufficient for him that man is recognized by the "genuine political theories" to be a "dangerous," "perilous," "dynamic being" (59, 61). For one thing, only in this way can he show that all truly political theories are *in harmony* with the truth of original sin, quite apart from the question of whether the respective theoreticians accept the dogma itself. But thus and only thus is Schmitt able to maintain that the relationship (which he conceives in "ontological and existential" terms) between theology and politics is foundational. Another advantage is that he can effectively demarcate his "mentality" from "moral theology" and make clear that the political theology he advocates is far from envisaging a "merely normative morals." Finally, the summary talk of "evil" man sufficiently blurs the differences between Schmitt's own anthropological position and those with quite another basis so as "to make" the specific meaning of Schmitt's anthropological confession of faith "*nearly* disappear," and to avoid exposing it too much with regard to both political and theological criticism.

59. Cf. Leo Strauss, *Hobbes' politische Wissenschaft*, pp. 18–36, and *What Is Political Philosophy?* pp. 176–81, 189–91.

No, it is not the "admiration of animal power" that causes Schmitt to emphasize man's dangerousness and in so doing to appeal to the most varied witnesses. After Strauss reproaches Schmitt for speaking "with an unmistakable *sympathy*, of the 'evil' that is not to be understood morally," and points out to Schmitt that this sympathy prevents him from remaining "in harmony with himself" (N26), Schmitt deletes a whole series of statements that could awaken that impression. Citations in which the "core of human nature" is formulated as "animality, drives, affects," or citations in which there is talk of the "play of affects" or of the "dignity of the power-type," are eliminated by this editing, as is the estimation of "Plessner's dynamic 'steadfast openness'" as being "nearer to 'evil' than to 'good' because of its positive relationship to danger and to the dangerous," and as are the remarks (which might very well unduly blur the contours of Schmitt's own position) that even Nietzsche belongs "on the side of 'evil'" and that "finally 'power' generally (according to the famous comment of Burckhardt, which incidentally is not unambiguous) is something evil" (59, 60). In place of all these statements, a direct rejoinder to the question raised by Strauss[60] appears: "It is self-evident, as Hobbes correctly emphasized, that a genuine enmity is possible only between human beings.[61] The political dis-

60. The change in the last sentence that precedes the new text of 1933 replies to Strauss (N26): "Here there is an immediate connection of political anthropology with what the seventeenth-century philosophers of the state (Hobbes, Spinoza, Pufendorff) called the 'state of nature' in which the states live among one another, a state of perpetual danger and endangering in which for that very reason the acting subjects are 'evil,' *that is, not pacified,* like animals that are moved by their drives, by hunger, greed, fear, jealousy, *and rivalries of every kind*" (III, 41–42). My emphasis.

61. Schmitt gives no information about which statement of Hobbes he has in view. In the *Theorie des Partisanen* he later refers expressly to *De Homine* X. 3 (Schmitt erroneously writes IX, 3): "Hobbes says: man is just as much more

tinction between friend and enemy is to the same degree deeper than all oppositions that exist in the animal world, as the extent to which man, as a being who exists spiritually, stands above the animal." For Schmitt the distinction between friend and enemy has nothing to do with the "rivalries of all kinds" (III, 42) that motivate animals, nothing to do with animality, and nothing at all to do with innocent evil. The oppositions between friend and enemy "are of a spiritual sort, as is all man's existence"; this statement, too, Schmitt inserts into the 1933 text (III, 9). More than two decades later he expresses the same core thought, which his "anthropology" orbits, as follows: "The dog does not call the very being of the cat into question spiritually or morally, and likewise the cat does not do so to the dog." Their opposition wholly contrasts with the enmity that prevails between men, which "nature does not" generate. For the enmity between men "contains a tension that far transcends what is natural."[62]

---

dangerous to other men by whom he believes himself endangered than is any animal, as the weapons of man are more dangerous than the so-called natural weapons of the animal, for example: teeth, claws, horns, or poison" (p. 95). Note the context in Hobbes.

62. *Die geschichtliche Struktur*, pp. 149, 150–51. Cf. *Ex Captivitate Salus*, pp. 68, 75, 78.

VI

Schmitt's answers constitute a whole, produce a complete picture, as soon as one perceives and bears in mind the unifying center to which they refer—in vaguer or more precise formulations, in more open or more hidden expressions—with ever new twists and turns. Schmitt replies to the cardinal question of the necessity of the political with various approaches and in various contexts. The first answer he gives is the most hidden and the most precise. It comprehends, in its result, everything else that Schmitt has to offer on the subject. It refers immediately to the passage in which Strauss for the first time directs the cardinal question to Schmitt, and in several respects one could call this answer the "most personal" of the replies to Strauss. Whether written "ad hominem" or not, it is at all events one of the most remarkable replies in the entire dialogue. The point of departure for the forceful discussion that Strauss culminates with the statement that, as long as man's dangerousness "is only believed in" the political is "in principle *threatened*" (N21), is furnished by Schmitt's statement: "Whether and when" the definitively depoliticized "state of the earth and of humanity will occur, I do not know. For the time being it does not exist. It would be a dishonest fiction[63] to assume that that state is now at hand" (54). On this statement Strauss comments that no one, and "least of all Schmitt himself," can "take relief in the fact that the depoliticized state *'for the time being* does not exist'" (N17). Schmitt's rhetorical "positivism" directs the reader's attention all the more certainly to the question of how things stand with the asserted inescapabil-

---

63. "It would be a fiction aiming at fraud to suppose it present today or tomorrow" (III, 36).

ity of the political. "In view of the fact that there is today
a powerful movement striving for the total elimination of
the real possibility of war and hence the abolition of the
political, in view of the fact that this movement not only
exercises a great influence upon the mentality of the age
but also authoritatively determines the real circumstances—this movement led, after all, to war's being 'today . . . probably neither something pious, nor something
morally good, nor something profitable' [36], whereas in
earlier centuries war could indeed be all these things—in
view of this fact one must look beyond today and ask:
granted that 'war as a real possibility is still present today,'
will war still be a possibility present tomorrow? or the day
after tomorrow?" (N17). Schmitt's answer is as succinct as
it is subtle. In the revised version of the *Concept of the
Political*, in the statement that war is "today . . . probably
neither something pious, nor something morally good, nor
something profitable," he replaces the word *today*, itali-
cized by Strauss, with the modifier "in an age that veils
its metaphysical oppositions in moral or economic terms"
(III, 18 f.).[64] War will be present as a real possibility not

64. Karl Löwith noticed the change but did not understand it as an answer to
Strauss's question. Thus he sees only an inconsistency, an odd contrast to his
imaginary picture of Schmitt's political decisionism, and he does not take the
contradiction as an opportunity to examine whether the image is correct. "The
possible meaning of war," Löwith comments on the new wording of 1933, "is
thus referred here—in reference to our time, also—to metaphysical oppositions,
although all Schmitt's arguments have their specifically polemical note precisely
in the denial of the theological, the metaphysical, the moral, and the economic
as authoritative for the properly political." "Politischer Dezisionismus," p. 113
n. —Schmitt had a notion of *how* Strauss read, and we have at our disposal
abundant illustrative material, all kinds of evidence, for how Schmitt himself
read; how, for example, he watched for the *decisive* sentence of a book or for the
one word that matters in a text. The way in which he carries on his dialogue
with Strauss is therefore anything but amazing. Schmitt later attempted another
discussion on the issue of Thomas Hobbes (see *Der Leviathan in der Staatslehre
des Thomas Hobbes*, pp. 20–21, 38), and in the final years of his life he was still
concerned with the question of whether Strauss "knew my book on the Leviathan

only tomorrow and the day after but up to "the end of time,"[65] because war is based on *metaphysical oppositions*. Metaphysical oppositions can be draped in moral or economic terms, but that does not blot them out of existence. Nothing human is capable of blotting them out. No man will be master of them. "Metaphysics is something unavoidable,"[66] and the "metaphysical core of all politics"[67] is the guarantor that political oppositions will be inescapable as long as metaphysical oppositions are unavoidable.

In a further respect Schmitt attempts to identify more pithily the locus of his own position by adumbrating its metaphysical anchorage and metaphysical meaning; his purpose is to secure his position against being misunderstood as having contended that the affirmation of the political (the affirmation that he opposes to negation of the political in his polemic against liberalism) has its meaning in the "affirmation of fighting as such, wholly irrespective of what is being fought *for*." Strauss expressed, with all the clarity one could possibly wish for, what the "affirmation of the political in disregard of the moral" and, we might add, in disregard of the theological, "would signify." "He

---

and, especially, whether he perceived the challenge of my essay on Hobbes 'Die vollendete Reformation' (that Jesus is the Christ)." In Schmitt's essay of 1965, Leo Strauss is never once mentioned. However, a footnote (p. 58) refers the reader to "the charming book of Samuel I. Mintz, *The Hunting of Leviathan* (Cambridge, 1962), which, by the way, sensibly opposes the current labeling of Hobbes as an atheist (p. 44)." A reader who follows the reference and turns to page 44 will find the relevant name there. (In the reprint of the essay in the appendix to the new edition of Schmitt's book on Hobbes [Cologne, 1982], the editor, the printer, or the proofreader, but in any case not Schmitt himself, deleted "p. 44." So the point of the reference is lost.) The answer to Schmitt's "challenge" can be found in the study "On the Basis of Hobbes's Political Philosophy" of 1954. (Leo Strauss, *What Is Political Philosophy?* pp. 182–91.) See n. 40 above and 101 below.

65. Cf. *Politische Theologie II*, p. 75.
66. *Politische Romantik*, p. 23.
67. *Politische Theologie*, p. 44 (65).

who affirms the political as such comports himself *neutrally* toward all groupings into friends and enemies." He "respects all who want to fight; he is just as *tolerant* as the liberals—but with the opposite intention: whereas the liberal respects and tolerates all '*honest*' convictions so long as they merely acknowledge the legal order, *peace*, as sacrosanct, he who affirms the political as such respects and tolerates all '*serious*' convictions, that is, all decisions oriented to the real possibility of *war*. Thus the affirmation of the political as such proves to be a liberalism with the opposite polarity" (N32). Strauss leaves no doubt that the affirmation of the political as such is *not* Schmitt's "last word" (N33, N29). But even if only his "first word against liberalism," in 1933 Schmitt no longer wants to have the affirmation of the political understood, or to let it exist, as an affirmation of fighting *irrespective of what is being fought for*. In the third edition he expressly distinguishes between two fundamentally different "attitudes" toward war, the "agonal" on one hand and the "political" on the other. He now separates "political opposition," the "genuine opposition between friend and enemy," from "agonal opposition," the "unpolitical, agonal contest" (III, 10, 12, 15, 17). To the passage in which he introduces the new distinction between enemy and opponent—"The opponent, the 'antagonist' in the bloody contest of the '*agon*,' is also not the enemy"—he adds a footnote, of which the first sentence reads: "A. Baeumler interprets the concept of battle of Nietzsche and Heraclitus entirely in terms of the agonal. Query: whence come the enemies in Valhalla?" In the center of the note, which is not exactly "suited to the time,"[68]

68. Schmitt is much more cautious in changing his statement about the political character of the oppositions that exist "*within* the state as an organized political unity." In 1932 he had written that "numerous *secondary* concepts of 'political'" arise there. "Yet here too an opposition and antagonism—relativized, to be sure,

Schmitt once again brings metaphysics into play. "The great metaphysical opposition of *agonal* and *political* thought arises in every more profound discussion of war. In most recent times I would cite the magnificent dispute between Ernst Jünger and Paul Adams (*Deutschlandsender*, Februar 1, 1933) . . . Here Ernst Jünger held the view of the agonal principle ('man is not designed for peace'), whereas Paul Adams saw the meaning of war in the establishment of dominion, order, and peace" (III, 10). In the controversy between Ernst Jünger and Paul Adams, Schmitt sides not with the "bellicose" nationalist but with the "authoritarian" Catholic. Leo Strauss is right: for Schmitt, the "ultimate quarrel occurs not between bellicosity and pacifism (or nationalism and internationalism)" (N25).[69] Strauss is likewise right in saying that Schmitt's last word is not the affirmation of the political in the sense of affirmation of fighting as such, but "the order of the human things" (95).[70] To Schmitt, fighting as little bears

by the existence of the state's political unity that comprehends all oppositions—within the state always remain constitutive for the concept of the political" (30). In 1933 he says instead: "Here the opposition between friend and enemy fades in importance, because oppositions within a political unity at peace are involved. *Admittedly*, here too an opposition and antagonism—relativized, to be sure, by the existence of the state's political unity that comprehends all oppositions—within the state always remain constitutive for the concept of the political. *But it remains open whether in such oppositions a merely 'agonal' competition that affirms the common unity is present, or whether the beginnings of a genuine friend-enemy opposition that negates the political unity, that is, a latent civil war, is already at hand*" (III, 12). My emphasis.

69. Cf. letter of September 4, 1932, page 125 below.

70. In 1934 Schmitt claimed to be the spokesman for a "mode of thought concerned with concrete order and formation," and he opposed this type of thought, as "a third kind of jurisprudential thought," to "normativism" and "decisionism." However, beyond general proclamations of the necessity of such thought ("Now a mode of thought concerned with concrete order and formation is needed, a type of thought that is adequate for the numerous new tasks arising from the situation of state, nation, economy, and ideology and for the new forms of community."), and beyond the repeatedly expressed hope that with recourse to general clauses "such as good manners, equity and faith, reasonable and unreasonable demand, important ground, etc.," "finally" this thought can "prevail"

its "purpose in itself" as does art. Neither are politics and war objects of an "aesthetic world view"[71] for Schmitt, nor do characterizations like "resoluteness for everything as well as for nothing" or formulas such as "decision in favor of decision" strike his "innermost core."[72] Schmitt is not a follower of Nietzsche,[73] and he exists in a "metaphysical opposition" to Ernst Jünger that becomes clear in their differing attitudes toward war but extends far beyond that difference.[74] As if the distinction between opponent and enemy, between the bloody contest of the *agon* and the "genuine" political opposition between friend and enemy,

---

(*Über die drei Arten des rechtswissenschaftlichen Denkens*, pp. 58, 59, 67; cf. 60, 63, and 66), Schmitt's "mode of thought concerned with concrete order," extended to, and in fact became *concrete* in, only the field of international law. This observation applies particularly to *Völkerrechtliche Großraumordnung mit Interventionsverbot für raumfremde Mächte. Ein Beitrag zum Reichsbegriff im Völkerrecht* (Berlin and Vienna, 1939; third and fourth editions, expanded and updated, 1941). At the end of the reprint of the final chapter of *Völkerrechtliche Großraumordung* in *Positionen und Begriffe* (p. 312) Schmitt in 1939 again takes up the citation from Virgil (*Ecloga* IV, 5) with which in 1929 the essay "Die europäische Kultur in Zwischenstadien der Neutralisierung" concluded and which he placed at the end of the *Concept of the Political: Ab integro nascitur ordo.*

71. Cf. *Politische Romantik*, pp. 21, 222.

72. *Ex Captivitate Salus*, pp. 52–53.

73. Schmitt treats Nietzsche with lifelong scant regard and brusque rejection. The sentence that concludes the main text of his new preface to *Politische Romantik* is: "One must see the three men whose distorted faces stare through the colorful romantic veil, Byron, Baudelaire, and Nietzsche, the three high priests and simultaneously the three sacrificial lambs of this private priesthood" (p. 27). Twenty-five years later he writes: "Nietzsche, full of fury, saw Hegel and the sixth—i.e. the historical—sense of the Germans as the great postponer on the path to open atheism." "Drei Möglichkeiten eines christlichen Geschichtsbildes," p. 930. Schmitt several times repeats this statement about Nietzsche, whom he seldom mentions in his writings, and he speaks no less than four times of his "fury" or "fit of fury"; see "Die andere Hegel-Linie," p. 2, *Verfassungsrechtliche Aufsätze*, pp. 428 and 429; earlier—and without the attribute "fury"—"Beschleuniger wider Willen oder: Problematik der westlichen Hemisphäre," in *Das Reich*, April 19, 1942. Cf. *Donoso Cortés*, pp. 98, 107, 109, 111–12.

74. Schmitt emphasizes anew the difference between their views of the political and of war in an article under the entry "Politics" in a reference book published in 1936: "The deepest opposition in the views of the essence of the political does

666 of 162

and as if the very statement that war can be "more or less war depending on the the degree of enmity," did not sufficiently emphasize that the concept of the political is for Schmitt something *different* from the affirmation of fighting as such and *very much more* is at stake than a "simple criterion" by which the enemy "is plainly the other, the stranger" (a criterion by which the reference "to the real possibility of physical killing" would virtually guarantee scientific implementability)—as if all the other "refinements" together were not adequate, Schmitt finally "refines" his view of the holy wars and crusades of the Church as well. In 1927 the rhetoric of "pure politics" had left no room for those. In 1932, Schmitt introduces them into the "sphere" of the political as "actions that, like other wars, are based upon a decision about the enemy." But only in 1933—of all times— does he formally concede that the holy wars and crusades of the Church "can be based on an especially genuine and profound decision about the enemy."[75]

Why does Schmitt keep his intentions obscure for so long? Why does he attempt to give the impression that he

---

not concern the question whether politics can relinquish all fighting or not (politics could not do so at all without ceasing to be politics), but the other question, *what war and fighting derive their meaning from.* Does war have its meaning in itself or in the peace that is to be achieved by war? According to the view of a pure "nothing [counts] but the spirit of the warrior," war has its meaning, its right, and its heroism in itself; man is, as Ernst Jünger says, 'not designed for peace.' The famous sentence of Heraclitus means the same thing: 'War is the father and king of all; some it proves to be gods, others to be men; of some it makes free men, of others, slaves.' Such a view is purely *warlike* in opposition to the *political* viewpoint. The latter rather supposes that wars are sensibly waged for the sake of peace and are a means of politics." Hermann Franke, ed., *Handbuch der neuzeitlichen Wehrwissenschaften,* vol. 1: *Wehrpolitik und Kriegführung* (Berlin and Leipzig, 1936), p. 549. —The *opposition of faith* by which Schmitt sees himself separated from Jünger is expressed much more clearly in the discussion, published by Schmitt in the *Festschrift für Ernst Jünger,* of the opposition of *historical uniqueness* and *eternal recurrence.* "Die geschichtliche Struktur," pp. 141, 146–54, 166, 167.

75. III, 30. Compare the revealing changes made in the preceding sentence in the second and third editions (I, 17; 48; III, 30).

intends only to describe "what is," as if it were enough for him that the political "for the time being" still exists? Why does he speak of "suppositions" where his deepest convictions are being discussed? Why does he take pains to conceal his moral judgment, his evaluative stance, toward the political? Strauss offers an explanation in response to the last question: Every evaluative stance toward the political would in Schmitt's eyes be "a 'free, unmonitorable decision that concerns no one other than the person who freely makes the decision'; it would essentially be a 'private matter' [49]; but the political is removed from all arbitrary, private discretion; it has the character of transprivate *obligation*. If it is now presupposed that all ideals are private and thus nonobligatory, obligation cannot be conceived as such, as duty, but can be conceived only as inescapable necessity. It is this presupposition, then, that disposes Schmitt to assert the inescapability of the political, and—as soon as his subject matter forces him to stop maintaining this assertion—to conceal his moral judgment; and this presupposition is, as he himself emphasizes, the characteristic presupposition of the 'individualistic-liberal society' [49]" (N31). But does Schmitt himself regard his stance toward the political as the position of a "person who freely makes the decision"? Is the presupposition that all ideals are nonobligatory his ultimate presupposition? Strauss's double attack, both his piercing inquiry into the necessity of the political and the criticism that Schmitt's thought remains decisively locked in the grip of liberalism, entices Schmitt to lower his reserve to the extent that the theological presuppositions come to light; and it is these presuppositions that *both* lead him to believe in the inescapability of the political *and* determine his moral judgment against any effort to set into motion the world without seriousness, the state of perfect, this-worldly security, universal business.

Why, then, it finally must be asked, why does Schmitt
take pains to conceal the theological presuppositions of his
politics? If we leave aside all personal or private and (in
the narrow sense) all historical or tactical considerations,
two reasons are decisive. In his opposition to liberalism,
Schmitt sees himself opposed to an enemy who "would
like to dissolve even metaphysical truth into a discussion."[76] Therefore Schmitt adopts the strategy of making
the "metaphysics" of liberalism the object of criticism, of
illuminating from the perspective of his political theology
the "consistent, comprehensive metaphysical system" of
liberalism, and of attacking "faith in discussion," without
exposing the core of his own politics to discussion, surren-
dering that core to "eternal conversation," or allowing it to
be taken in and relativized by the "eternal competition of
opinions."[77] In this strategy Schmitt is heedful of a saying
of Bruno Bauer's that he particularly admired: "Only he
can conquer who knows his prey better than it knows itself."[78] The second, theological reason is intimately connected with the political reason. Carl Schmitt envelops the
center of his thought in darkness because the center of his
thought is faith. The center is faith in God's having become man, in "a historical event of infinite, unpossessable,
unoccupiable uniqueness."[79] The things of revelation,
however, are unsuited for discussion with unbelievers. In

76. *Politische Theologie*, p. 54 (80).
77. *Die geistesgeschichtliche Lage*, pp. 45–46, 58, 61.
78. *Positionen und Begriffe*, p. 293. Cf. *Der Nomos der Erde*, p. 102; *Ex Captivitate Salus*, pp. 18, 39. In addition to Bauer's text cited in *Positionen und Begriffe*, namely, *Die bürgerliche Revolution in Deutschland seit dem Anfang der deutsch-katholischen Bewegung bis zur Gegenwart* (Berlin, 1849), p. 294, see *Die theologische Erklärung der Evangelien* (Berlin, 1852), pp. 35 ff.
79. "Drei Möglichkeiten," p. 930; cf. *Ex Captivitate Salus*, pp. 12, 45, 52–53, 61, 68, 75, 78; *Der Nomos der Erde*, p. 14; *Theorie des Partisanen*, p. 26; "Nach-wort" to J. A. Kanne, *Aus meinem Leben* (Berlin, 1940; first published in 1918), p. 68.

such matters arguments make no difference. For what counts here is exclusively "the truth, not irrefutability," that is, the truth of *faith*.[80]

Schmitt believes himself to be obligated. He does not conceive of himself as someone acting in the service of a "free decision" that concerns him alone. He believes himself under an obligation to engage in *political action*. But the obligation that he accepts as binding is the obligation of *his* faith. Leo Strauss's critique "overlooks" what is decisive for Schmitt. The critique sees precisely the only thing that has weight for Strauss and not only for him. Schmitt cannot understand the obligatoriness of the political in any other way than as fate. The sole salvation he can see from the relativism of "private matters" is the authoritative power of revelation and of Providence. For him the truth of revelation is such a certain source of "pure and whole knowledge" that only a subordinate, derivative significance can be ascribed to any efforts to attain by human means knowledge of the nature of man and valid statements about the character of the political. If what is most important is irreversibly settled, striving for knowledge will, at best, result in confirmation of what was already "known." In view of the truth of original sin, for example, everything that anthropology can bring to light remains secondary. The "suppositions" of anthropology may be "interesting." They are not decisive. Therefore Schmitt does not need to entertain the "question of the natural qualities of man" (65). For the same reason, Schmitt does not make his conception of the political depend on a primary tendency of human nature to form exclusive groups. For him, the political is not destiny in the peculiar sense that "the tendency to separate

80. Cf. "Die Sichtbarkeit der Kirche," p. 71; *Politische Theologie*, p. 52 (74); *Politische Romantik*, p. 137.

(and therewith the grouping of humanity into friends and enemies) is given with *human nature*."[81]

The political is destiny because it keeps men, whether they are willing or not, in the condition of historicity and Judgment; because it takes men beyond their private intentions into great events in which "spirit fights against spirit, life fights life" (95); and because it causes men, whether or not they are aware of it, to participate in "an implantation of the eternal into the course of time—an implantation that roars in grand testimonies and grows in powerful creaturings."[82] In all transformations of his political doctrine, in all changes in the concept of the political, for Schmitt the political remains *essentially* fate. Whether the political is articulated from the perspective of war or with a view to civil war, whether it is articulated offensively as the most extreme degree of intensity or defensively as the ultimate domain of retreat, what always matters decisively to Schmitt is searching out the inevitable in the political and bringing to bear the *objective power* of the enemy, the power that keeps world history in motion; and bringing to bear the question that the individual does not have the arbitrary discretion to ask—the question that *is* the enemy. Schmitt believes he can recognize in the enemy the tool of Providence. Great political formations and figures, the state, the empire, or the guerrilla, may suffice for the "unique" historical "call" or fall short of it; they may for a certain time, for *their* time, establish orders and finally fail; but, by means of the enmities that are effective in them and are produced by them, "the dark meaning of our history grows on."[83] The enemy imperiously demands an

81. Leo Strauss, letter of September 4, 1932, page 125 below. My emphasis.
82. "Drei Möglichkeiten," p. 931.
83. *Ex Captivitate Salus*, pp. 89–90; "Die geschichtliche Struktur," pp. 147–52, 166; "Drei Möglichkeiten," p. 930; cf. *Positionen und Begriffe*, p. 239, and

answer. There is no escaping him, for "the genuine enemy cannot be deceived." For Schmitt, the enemy is the guarantor of the seriousness of life. He is so to such an extent that Schmitt would rather be the enemy of him who has no enemy than have no enemy. "Woe to him who has no *enemy*, for *I* will be his enemy at the Last Judgment."[84]

"Gespräch über den Partisanen," in Joachim Schickel, ed., *Guerilleros, Partisanen. Theorie und Praxis* (Munich, 1970), p. 23. Schmitt in 1942 concludes his text *Land und Meer. Eine weltgeschichtliche Betrachtung* by expressing confidence that "the new *nomos* of our planet is growing inexorably and irresistibly." "Only in battle can the new *nomos* arise. Many will see only death and destruction in it. Some believe they are experiencing the end of the world. In reality we are experiencing only the end of the previous relationship of land and sea. But human fear of what is new is often just as great as the fear of emptiness, even though what is new is the overcoming of emptiness. Therefore, those multitudes see only meaningless disorder where in reality a new meaning is struggling for its order. The old *nomos* admittedly no longer applies, and with it goes a whole system of received measures, norms, and relationships. But what is coming is not yet therefore only boundlessness or a *nomos*-hostile nothingness. Even in the cruel war of old and new powers, just measures arise and meaningful proportions form. / Here, too, gods are and rule / Great is their measure." (Leipzig, 1942, p. 76; cf. second, altered edition [Stuttgart, 1954], p. 63.)

84. *Ex Captivitate Salus*, p. 90.

VII

Strauss understands Schmitt's polemic against liberalism as a "concomitant or preparatory action." That polemic "is to clear the field for the battle of decision" that occurs only between mortal enemies, "between the 'spirit of technicity,' the 'mass faith that inspires an antireligious, thisworldly activism' [93], and the opposite spirit and faith, which, as it seems, still has no name. Ultimately, two completely opposed answers to the question of what is right, confront each other, and these answers allow of no mediation and no neutrality (cf. the remark about 'twomembered antitheses' and 'three-membered diagrams' or 'constructions' on p. 73)" (N33). Is liberalism not a real enemy to Schmitt, and Schmitt not a genuine enemy of liberalism? Certainly, "what *ultimately* matters to Schmitt is not the battle against liberalism"; but in the battle of *faith* against *faith*, is liberalism's role merely that of a "neutral" who impairs "the view of the enemy" and is waved aside with a sweep of the hand "in order to gain a free line of fire" (N33)? Is liberalism not the driving force in the broad movement of "antireligious, this-worldly activism"? Is liberalism not the protagonist of the "great metaphysical construction and interpretation of history" that proclaims to humanity linear progress "from fanaticism to spiritual freedom and spiritual coming of age, from dogma to criticism, from superstition to enlightenment, from darkness to light" (72)? Does liberalism not stand in the service of that "activistic metaphysics" that inscribed on its banners the faith "in the unlimited 'shrinking of natural limits,' in the unlimited possibilities of the natural, this-worldly existence of man for change and happiness" (93)? In the third edition of the *Concept of the Political*, Schmitt stresses the weight that he attributes to liberalism as the enemy of the political. Liberalism figures in that edition as the "new faith" that puts its stake in, and makes every effort to achieve, the eventual "victory" of economy, industry, and technology over state, war, and politics (III, 56). "One can regard the year 1814 as the year in which this new faith was born, the year in which England triumphed over the military imperialism of Napoleon." The new faith is the "turn to the economic," the working toward the victory of the "industrial, commercial society," the ideology that not politics but the economy is destiny—Walther Rathenau against Napoleon Bonaparte.[85] Schmitt shows how very seriously he takes liberalism as his enemy by subsuming Marxism under liberalism. "Marxism is only a case of the application of the liberal mentality of the nineteenth century" (III, 55–56). The Marxists of today are the bourgeois of the day after tomorrow. Liberalism and Marxism alike have set the "final war of humanity" before the definitive establishment of universal peace and security. *Ultimately* both derive from *one* faith.[86] The synopsis of liberalism and

85. "The often cited saying of Walther Rathenau . . . that today not politics but the economy is destiny. This saying served a political power that is based on economic positions" (III, 60; cf. 76).

86. III, 55, 58, 61. Cf. *Der Leviathan in der Staatslehre des Thomas Hobbes*, p. 63; "Die letzte globale Linie" in *Völker und Meere* (Leipzig, 1943), pp. 347–49; "Die Einheit der Welt," pp. 2, 7, 8–9; "Nehmen, Teilen, Weiden" (1953) in *Verfassungsrechtliche Aufsätze*, pp. 495–96, 503–4. —Schmitt's opposition to the *one* faith that joins liberalism and Marxism, as well as the significance of that faith for him down through his latest writings, is expressed especially clearly in two statements of 1952 and 1959: "The masses have a *religion of technicity*, and every technological progress appears to them to be at the same time a perfection of man himself, a direct step to the *earthly paradise* of the *one world*. Their evolutionary *credo* constructs a direct line of the ascent of humanity. Man, biologically and by nature an altogether weak being in need of help, creates for himself through technology a *new world* in which he is the strongest, indeed the *sole* being. The dangerous question that is necessarily connected to this increase in technological means, namely the question of where—on which men—the enor-

Marxism gives Strauss an answer to his explicit reference
to the significance of "two-membered antitheses." At the
same time, Schmitt leaves no doubt that he, on his own—
unlike Marxism, which follows "the liberal-bourgeois opponent onto the domain of the economic and there stands
him at bay, so to speak, in his own country and with his
own weapons" (III, 55)—determines, in an act of sovereign self-assertion, the level on which he meets the enemy:
The enemy will be located on the level of *faith*, he will be
identified with a view to his "metaphysics." In 1933 there
is talk not only of the "new faith" but also of the "metaphysics, disguised as 'science,' of the liberal nineteenth century," and likewise of the "complete inventory" of the "liberal catechism" that occurs in Benjamin Constant's 1814 text
on the *esprit de conquête* (III, 56, 57, 58). The author of that
work is no longer called "the inaugurator" but is now described as "a *Church Father* of the entire liberal spirituality of
the nineteenth century."[87] As for Karl Marx, Schmitt's text

mous power over other men is concentrated, may not be asked . . . *Eastern and
Western faith* flow together here." ("Die Einheit der Welt," pp. 8–9. With the
exceptions of *"one world"* and *"credo,"* my emphasis.) "Everything on our earth
today, in the East as well as in the West, that appeals to progress and development contains as its core a concrete and precise *credo*, of which the *principles of
faith* are as follows: The industrial revolution leads to an immense increase in
production; as a consequence of the increase in production, taking becomes
old-fashioned and even criminal; even sharing is, in view of the affluence, no
longer a problem; thus now there is only grazing, now there is only the *unproblematic happiness of pure consumption.* There are no longer wars and crises because
unchained production will no longer be partial and one-sided but total and global.
In other words: humanity would finally have found its formula, just as bees find
their formula in the beehive. *Things administer themselves; humanity encounters itself;*
wandering in the deserts of alienation has ended. In a *world that is created by men*
for men—and sometimes unfortunately also against men—man can *give* without
taking." ("Nomos-Nahme-Name," p. 102. With the exceptions of *"give"* and
"taking," my emphasis.)
    87. III, 56. My emphasis. Schmitt continues: "His treatise of 1814 already
contains the whole spiritual arsenal of this century that was filled with illusion
and fraud."

says that Marx "inserted" the idea that world history is a history of economic class struggle—"which many historians and philosophers had already said"—into the "idea of progress and development that is harbored in the philosophy of history, and therewith *drove* his idea of history *into the metaphysical and up to the most extreme political efficacy.*"[88] The enemy may explain what he will; he may turn and twist as he will; but the terrain on which Schmitt meets him is the terrain of political theology.[89] The confrontation occurs here. And here there are no "neutral parties."

The battle on the ground of political theology allows Schmitt a game *à deux mains*. Like "all political concepts," political theology for Schmitt has a "polemical meaning" and, at first, has a "concrete opposition in view" (31). Schmitt takes the concept from Bakunin, who had hurled it against Mazzini.[90] Schmitt adopts as his own what was intended, under the battle cry *Ni Dieu ni maître*, as an indictment by the Russian anarchist; he does so in order to reply to what appears to him to be the most extreme attack on theology and politics, with the most emphatic affirmation of both. The "concrete opposition" with a view to which Schmitt defines his position by means of the concept "political theology" is opposition to Bakunin, the opposition of authority to anarchy, of faith in revelation to atheism, of the defense of the theological, of the moral, and of

---

88. III, 55. My emphasis.

89. The concept itself is mentioned a single time in the second edition, namely within the "Rede über das Zeitalter der Neutralisierungen" (p. 89). In the third edition, which does not include the "Zeitalter der Neutralisierungen," Schmitt makes sure that the concept occurs in another passage "in passing" and thus remains present in the book (III, 23).

90. *La Théologie politique de Mazzini et l'Internationale* (St. Imier, 1871). Needless to say, Schmitt conveys nothing about the derivation of the concept and does not specifically call to the attention of those readers of *Politische Theologie* who fail to detect it by themselves the connection between the title of the text and the name of the enemy most keenly opposed by the book. Cf. n. 54 above.

the political idea against the paralysis "of all moral and political decisions in a paradisiacal, secular world of immediate, natural life and unproblematical carnality."[91][TN5] Of course, the foregoing statement does not mean that the concept has solely, even mainly, enmity toward anarchism "in view," or that the concept is bound to that enmity polemically. *Political theology* is the apt and only appropriate description of *Schmitt's teaching.* At the same time, the concept serves as a universally employable *weapon.* On one hand, political theology marks Schmitt's place in the political battle of faith, and, on the other hand, political theology is the instrument he uses like a virtuoso to force his opponent to participate in this battle. For Schmitt certainly does

91. *Politische Theologie,* p. 55 (82). "Only Bakunin endows the battle against theology with the logical consistency of an absolute naturalism" (p. 55 [81]; cf. pp. 45, 49, 56 [64–65, 69, 83–84]). At the end of *Römischer Katholizismus* (which, as he notes in *Politische Theologie,* he wrote "at the same time" as the latter "in March 1922") Schmitt places a consideration of the Catholic attitude toward Bakunin's anarchism and toward the association that "the industrial proletariat engaged in class struggle and Russiandom as it turns away from Europe" have entered into in the "Russian republic of soviets": "I know that more Christianity can lie in the Russian hatred of western European education than in liberalism and in German Marxism, that great Catholics regarded liberalism as a more terrible enemy than open, socialist atheism, and that ultimately, perhaps, the strength for a new form that would shape even the economic-technological age could potentially lie in formlessness. *Sub specie* of its duration that outlives everything else, here too the Catholic Church does not need to decide; here too it will be the *complexio* of all that survives. The Church is the heir. But there is nevertheless an unavoidable decision for the present day, for the current constellation, and for the present generation. Here the Church, even if it cannot declare itself in favor of any of the battling parties, really must take a side, as for example, in the first half of the nineteenth century, it took the side of the counterrevolutionaries. And here I believe that in that outlying battle of Bakunin the Catholic Church and the Catholic concept of humanity were on the side of the idea and of western European civilization, next to Mazzini and not next to the atheistic socialism of the anarchistic Russian" (pp. 79–80. The second edition reads: ". . . closer to Mazzini than to the atheistic socialism of the anarchistic Russian," p. 53.) Cf. *Römischer Katholizismus,* pp. 74–78 (49–51); *Die Diktatur: Von den Anfängen des modernen Souveränitätsgedankens bis zum proletarischen Klassenkampf* (Munich and Leipzig, 1921), p. 147; *Die geistesgeschichtliche Lage,* pp. 79, 83, 87; *Donoso Cortés,* pp. 9–10.

not use the term "political theology" merely for a political doctrine that, like his own, claims to be anchored in theology;[92] rather, he manages to trace "political theologies" even where any theology is expressly rejected, the political is negated, and all political theology is declared to have been "disposed of." Neither denial nor indifference provides the opponent an exit to escape the level of political theology. Either the opposed positions are based on "transfers" and "shifts" borrowed from theology; or they prove to be forms and products of "secularization"; or they have put themselves in the wrong by defecting from Christian theology; or they are passed off as metaphysics *malgré lui* and in this way stripped of their potential superiority— whether rational or natural, whether based on the philosophy of history or however else grounded to the position of faith in revelation.[93] Schmitt's political theology, its "pure and whole knowledge" regarding the "metaphysical core of all politics," provides the theoretical basis for a battle in which faith can always meet only faith. Political theology thus proves in one stroke its value both as Schmitt's weapon and as a strategy for disarming his opponent. If

92. Cf. *Politische Theologie*, pp. 37, 40, 45, [49, 56, 64]. In 1950 Schmitt declared: "I have now been advised that, because of the Christian dogma of the Trinity, a political theology has become impossible. I believe it without further ado." That he *by no means* believes it he demonstrates *ad oculos* throughout the entire book in which this sentence occurs (*Donoso Cortés*, p. 10). Twenty years later, Schmitt not only defends political theology in great detail against the "legend of its destruction" but is willing to drive political theology into the "core of the teaching of the Trinity" itself (*Politische Theologie II*, pp. 116–23).

93. Schmitt acts just like Donoso Cortés, who "in his radical spirituality," as Schmitt says, "always sees only the theology of the opponent." *Politische Theologie*, p. 54 [79]. Compare, along with frequent evidence, which can be increased almost at will, in the text and in the footnotes, *Politische Romantik*, pp. 23, 86, 87, 91, 223; *Die geistesgeschichtliche Lage*, pp. 41, 45–46, 64, 89; "Staatsethik und pluralistischer Staat," *Positionen und Begriffe*, p. 135; "Die vollendete Reformation," pp. 52, 61–63; *Politische Theologie II*, pp. 34–35, 124–26; "Die legale Weltrevolution," *Der Staat*, vol. 17, no. 3 (1978), p. 337.

"every utterance on the spiritual level has, consciously or unconsciously, a dogma—orthodox or heretical—as its premise,"[94] then only the decision between orthodoxy and heresy remains. He who does not accept the necessity of this decision thereby decides against orthodoxy and makes himself known as a heretic. It is no mere expression of cheap polemics when, for example, Schmitt calls Marx the "heresiarch of atheistic socialism" or the "true cleric of economic thought."[95] It is typical of the logical rigor of Schmitt's "ontological-existential mentality" to state that Bakunin *had to* become "the theologian of the anti-theological."[96] And it is no paradox but, on the contrary, in perfect harmony with Schmitt's political theology when he later attacks as a "religion of technicity" (93, 94) what he describes as an "antireligion of technicity" (80). It is a *religion* of technicity because, and to the extent that, it is an *anti*religion. The antireligion of technicity has a religious meaning. The "faith in technology" is not neutral. It is based on turning away from the true religion. Just as Bakunin was far from free to become absorbed in the carnality of the paradisiacal, secular world, so atheism emphatically had to be and to remain heretical faith, and the decision for or against God can by no means be avoided through a flight into a "system of infallible objectivity."[97] After the process of neutralizations and depoliticizations has reached its end, it turns out that the battlefield that one wished to abandon at the beginning of that process was never really left

94. *Politische Romantik*, p. 5.
95. "Der unbekannte Donoso Cortés" (1929), in *Donoso Cortés*, p. 74. Cf. *Die geistesgeschichtliche Lage*, pp. 64, 65, 67, 68, 71, 75.
96. *Politische Theologie*, 2d ed., p. 84. In the first edition the last two words—which are at the same time the final words of the text—are not yet "*werden mußte*," "had to become," but "*geworden ist*," "has become" (p. 56). Cf. "Die Sichtbarkeit der Kirche," p. 80.
97. *Römischer Katholizismus*, p. 31 (21).

behind. True, the quarrel was successfully transferred, in a "gradation of shifting central domains" (80), from theology to economics, seemingly ever farther toward the periphery. But as soon as the final "grade" of the process has been reached, as soon as the quarrel encroaches upon modern technology, which is no longer capable of holding out the prospect of any other neutrality than the neutrality of weapons that technology supplies for the battle, as soon as all detours have been taken and all retouchings have been washed away, the basic text comes into keen focus, the existential decision between friend and enemy makes its appearance, and the core of the quarrel emerges. Technology makes it become manifest that now, as before, at the end as at the beginning of the neutralization and depoliticization, religion opposes religion, faith fights faith, and "world history" remains "in motion." "The spirit of technicity that has led to the mass faith of an antireligious, this-worldly activism, is spirit—perhaps an evil and devilish spirit but something not to be dismissed as mechanistic and not to be included in technology." "It is the conviction of an activist metaphysics"; "one can call" the faith of this metaphysics "fantastic and Satanic, but not simply dead or spiritless, nor can one call it a mechanized soullessness" (93). Satan has no power over Providence and cannot avoid serving its purposes. World history is not yet at an end. The "heresiarch of atheistic socialism" and the "theologian of the antitheological" also, contribute to "the further growth" of world history's "dark meaning." No choice remains for the enemies of political theology but to attest to its truth.

Political theology seems unconquerable; it seems to have been sentenced to conquer. But what is the point of a victory if defeat is excluded, if—as a "theologian" highly esteemed by Schmitt remarked a human lifespan prior to the *Political Theology*—victory in faith has been placed into one's hand long in advance? Is the courage that political theology demands the courage of the man who lines up for battle *although* he knows that he has already won the victory? But whom must he fight, against whom must he first line up? Where is the real enemy? Behind what masks does he conceal himself? How can he be known? Political theology defends the primacy of action against knowledge, because political theology places everything under the commandment to be obedient. Political theology obtains its justification as a theory by "reviving lively oppositions and grouping the warring opponents as lively enemies,"[98] by forcing people to take sides in the quarrel of faith against faith, and by answering to the "concrete call of history" by joining the battle with a polemical doctrine of the political and maintaining awareness of the inescapability of the political. The most urgent task of political theology consists in concentrating all forces on the decision "that alone matters." Regarding when, where, and against whom this decision must be made, however, political theology cannot specify anything. It cannot prescribe any particular taking of sides or give action a "concrete" orientation, for the paths of Providence are unfathomable. The most important decision remains in every respect a matter of faith. One could say: political theology stops here, and the political theologian is wholly in his own realm. Is one to suppose that the decision born of the obedience of faith in the supreme authority cannot, in the end, be distinguished from the decision that bases one's commitment on nothing?[TN6] In the case of Carl Schmitt, everything depends on the answer to this question.[99] Inasmuch as his political theology is constructed on the peak of faith, *probity* has to

98. Cf. *Die geistesgeschichtliche Lage*, p. 85.
99. Cf. *Ex Captivitate Salus*, pp. 87–89, 52–53; *Politische Romantik*, pp. 25, 104.

carry the whole burden. More burdensome than the weight of the "theoretical" and practical decisions that political theology loads upon the political theologian is the relief it offers him in the very same decisions by means of the certainty that the course of fate is always *in order* already and that *salvation* is the meaning of all world history.[100]— Illusory as the supposed strength of political theology is, Schmitt's intelligence report on the enemy is equally unclear. As Strauss states, the battle of decision occurs solely between the mortal enemies. Apparently it has to be waged against the "mass faith of an antireligious, this-worldly activism" (N33). But in what figure: in the figure of bolshevism or that of liberalism? Is the "new faith" the mortal enemy, or does the "secular confrontation" with Judaism, which from the very beginning denies that "Jesus is the Christ," take precedence?[101] Might it be possible that with the advent of National Socialism the Antichrist has appeared on the stage, or has he long acted in concealment? In the event that the battle of decision still lies in the distant future and that what matters here and now is, short of the eschatological confrontation, to strengthen the *kat-*

100. *Über die drei Arten des rechtswissenschaftlichen Denkens*, pp. 25–26; *Politische Romantik*, p. 137; *Ex Captivitate Salus*, p. 53; *Land und Meer*, p. 58 (49). Cf. "Drei Möglichkeiten," p. 928; "Die geschichtliche Struktur," p. 147; also Schmitt's statements about war as God's judgment in "Totaler Feind, totaler Krieg, totaler Staat," *Positionen und Begriffe*, p. 239, as well as in *Ex Captivitate Salus*, p. 58. See nn. 83 and 91 above.

101. *Disputation über den Rechtsstaat*, pp. 86–87; "Eröffnung der wissenschaftlichen Vorträge durch den Reichsgruppenwalter Staatsrat Prof. Dr. Carl Schmitt," in *Das Judentum in der Rechtswissenschaft. Ansprachen, Vorträge, und Ergebnisse der Tagung der Reichsgruppe Hochschullehrer des NSRB. am 3. und 4. Oktober 1936*, no. 1, *Die deutsche Rechtswissenschaft im Kampf gegen den jüdischen Geist* (Berlin, 1936), p. 14 (cf. "Schlußwort," p. 30, 33, 34); "Die vollendete Reformation," pp. 62–63. Cf. *Der Leviathan in der Staatslehre des Thomas Hobbes*, pp. 88–89, 92–93, 108–10; *Land und Meer*, p. 10 (altered in the second edition, p. 8) and p. 67 (likewise altered in the second edition, p. 56; on what Disraeli "said about Judaism and Christianity," see Bruno Bauer, *Disraelis romantischer und Bismarcks sozialistischer Imperialismus* [Chemnitz, 1882], p. 53).

echon[102] that can subdue the Antichrist for an unknown period, how can the *restrainer* be distinguished from the hastener, and from the *hastener in spite of himself?* If the enemy is our own question as a figure, is Schmitt's figure not "unambiguously" determined?[103] Or might the identity of the political theologian be interchangeable with that of his real enemy?—Schmitt called himself a *Christian Epimetheus.*[104] The Christian Epimetheus believes that he is familiar with the *"arcanum* of ontology" and that he knows

102. Second Letter to Thessalonians, 2:6 and 7; Augustine, *De civitate dei,* XX, 19. "I do not believe that for an original Christian faith an image of history other than the *Kat-echon* is at all possible." *Der Nomos der Erde,* p. 29. Cf. pp. 28–36; *Land und Meer,* pp. 11–12, 56 (10, 47); "Beschleuniger wider Willen," in *Das Reich,* April 19, 1942; *Ex Captivitate Salus,* p. 31; "Drei Möglichkeiten," pp. 929–30; *Verfassungsrechtliche Aufsätze,* pp. 385, 428–29; *Politische Theologie II,* p. 81.

103. *Theorie des Partisanen,* p. 87; *Ex Captivitate Salus,* pp. 89–90. Cf. "Clausewitz als politischer Denker. Bemerkungen und Hinweise," in *Der Staat,* vol. 6, no. 4 (1967), pp. 495, 499. The expression (repeatedly used by Schmitt without any reference to its source) "The enemy is our own question as a figure" comes from the "Sang an Palermo" by the poet Theodor Däubler: "The enemy is our own question as a figure / And he will hunt us, as we will him to the same end." *Hymne an Italien* (Leipzig, 1919, 2d ed), p. 65. (See *Ex Captivitate Salus,* pp. 49, 53.)

104. *Ex Captivitate Salus,* pp. 12, 53; cf. p. 31. Note especially p. 89, and see *Politische Theologie II,* pp. 124–26. In 1933 the Catholic writer Konrad Weiss published a Christian-Marian interpretation of history entitled *Der christliche Epimetheus* (Verlag Edwin Runge, city omitted), to which Schmitt is referring with his self-characterization. In a note in *Der christliche Epimetheus,* Weiss turns to "the political and public reputation of Catholic teacher of law Carl Schmitt," "whose sense of law appears to be a mystical-practical, pure and whole thing, whereby the ambi-geneity of the logical-humane and always ultimately Christian, nonredisclosable position is to veer into the judicial decision and is to be led out into political-historical, spacious fruitfulness. This veering between law and mass, 'technology' and creature also appears as a specifically Catholic form of meaning of the present" (p. 81 n.). The friend's book also includes the sentence "salvation is, in opposition to all concepts, the decisive meaning of history" (p. 47); Schmitt makes this sentence his own in his "Weltgeschichtliche Betrachtung," and the remark may be described as the core and key sentence of his view of history (*Land und Meer,* p. 58; 2d ed., p. 49). On the theology of history by Weiss, which strongly influenced Schmitt, cf. pp. 12, 17, 21, 23, 28–29, 31, 34, 39, 54, 57, 78, 88–89, 101, 105, 109–10, 111.

that all historical truth is true only once. He believes he knows that "every human word is an answer," that every theory answers a unique signal, that the answer to the call of history "as seen by man can be only an anticipation— and even for the most part only a blind one—of a commandment that is to be obeyed."[105] Schmitt seeks to have the *Concept of the Political*, too, understood in the sense of an anticipation of a commandment, as the action of a Christian Epimetheus in the state of historicity and of the Judgment. When he declares that "all spirit is only spirit of the present" (79), that "all concepts of the spiritual sphere, including the concept of spirit, are in themselves pluralistic and can be understood only through an understanding of concrete political existence" (84), and that "all political concepts, ideas, and words have a *polemical* meaning" (31), he is responding to a unique signal that he believes he hears as a call.[106] What separates the historicism of the Christian Epimetheus from the historicism of a Croce or a Collingwood[107] is the "pure and whole knowledge" about the meaning and fate of the drama that keeps world history in motion. What alone separates, but certainly does separate, Schmitt's historicism from the historicism of his liberal contemporaries is Schmitt's faith.

Leo Strauss does not have the horizon of faith in view when at the end of his "Notes" he says that the "criticism of liberalism introduced" by the author of the *Concept of the*

---

105. "Die geschichtliche Struktur," p. 148, 151, 166. Cf. "Drei Möglichkeiten," pp. 930–31; *Der Nomos der Erde*, pp. 6, 20.

106. *Politische Theologie*, p. 55 (82); cf. Preface to the Second Edition, p. 7; *Staat, Bewegung, Volk*, p. 17; *Politische Theologie II*, pp. 25 and 73.

107. On Croce, see "Die europäische Kultur in Zwischenstadien der Neutralisierung," p. 517 (cf. *Concept of the Political*, 79); on Collingwood, see "Die geschichtliche Struktur," pp. 151–54. Compare the criticism by Leo Strauss in "On Collingwood's Philosophy of History," in *Review of Metaphysics*, vol. 5, no. 4 (June 1952), pp. 559–86.

Political can "be completed only if one succeeds in gaining a horizon beyond liberalism" (N35). But of what import is the completion of this critique, which cannot be achieved in the horizon of liberalism itself and is not possible without a fundamental questioning of the theoretical presuppositions of liberalism? It is not so much the crisis of liberalism—which, as Strauss remarks in 1935, "has recently come into disrepute partly for very good and partly for very bad reasons"—but, to a far greater extent, the fact that the "systematics of liberal thought" in Europe "has still not been replaced by any other system," that makes the confrontation with liberalism the task and point of departure of a venture that is *ultimately* not concerned with the critique of liberalism. The critique of the present "is the necessary beginning, the constant companion, and the sure mark of the search for truth as that search is possible in our age."[108] The ascent from opinion to knowledge, the striving to liberate oneself from the cave of historical existence in order to reach the light of a pure and whole knowledge—the striving that is the original meaning of philosophizing—has to start with the most powerful opinions of the age and question its strongest prejudices. Thus, the critique of liberalism in general, and of the liberal concept of culture in particular, is for Strauss part of a train of thought guided by the requirement (which grows out of the critique itself) to seek a further, more comprehensive horizon beyond liberalism. Strauss pioneers his path of "return to the origin" (N34) as a path of revival of supposedly obsolete, "historically decided" controversies. Starting from the challenge of the deepest conviction of the present—that all thought, understanding, and action are historical, that is, have no other ground than groundless human

108. Leo Strauss, *Philosophie und Gesetz*, pp. 9–10, 13.

decision or the dispensation of fate, and that accordingly we are denied any possibility of understanding thinkers of the past as they understood themselves—and then attempting to get to the bottom of the quarrel between enlightenment and orthodoxy[109] and to resume the subject matter dealt with in that quarrel, the path finally leads to the renewal of the *querelle des anciens et des modernes*. The task required for a "radical critique of liberalism" and regarded by Strauss as "urgent"—namely, to reach an "appropriate understanding of Hobbes"—makes it imperative to regain the horizon in which Hobbes "completed the foundation of liberalism" (N35); hence the task leads to the incomparably more difficult enterprise of advancing to that "turning point and vortex of so-called world history," Socrates, in order to reach a philosophically appropriate understanding of the founder of political philosophy and

---

109. "A critical examination of the arguments and counterarguments that have been advanced in this quarrel leads to the result that a refutation of the 'externally' understood basic assertions of the tradition is out of the question. For all these assertions rest on the irrefutable presupposition that God is almighty, that His will is unfathomable. If God is almighty, miracles and revelation in general and, in particular, the miracles and the revelation of the Bible are possible . . . But although the attack of the Enlightenment on orthodoxy has failed, the battle between the two hostile powers has nonetheless had a momentous positive result for the Enlightenment: the Enlightenment has succeeded, provisionally, as one may say in defending itself on its part against the attack of orthodoxy. If the Enlightenment was unable to prove the possibility or the unreality of miracles—to give an example that is more than an example—it could show the unknowability of the miracle as such and thereby protect itself against the claims of orthodoxy. Thus what applies to the aggressive critique advanced by the Enlightenment does not apply to its defensive critique. By means of the quarrel between the Enlightenment and orthodoxy it became clearer and better known than it had been before that the presuppositions of orthodoxy—the reality of creation, miracles, and revelation—are not known (philosophically or historically) but only believed in, and thus do not have the peculiar obligatoriness of what is known." Leo Strauss, *Philosophie und Gesetz*, pp. 18, 19–20; cf. pp. 13–15. Note especially pp. 27–28 and *Liberalism Ancient and Modern* (New York, 1968), p. 256. See *Persecution and the Art of Writing*, pp. 105–7, and n. 41 above.

of what he set into motion.[110] The new orientation inaugu-
rated by renouncing the prejudice that going behind modern thought is out of the question found its first expression,
according to Strauss's own testimony, "not entirely by accident" in the "Notes."[111] The question of Socrates was *from
the very beginning* the decisive, fundamental question for
Strauss. Led by that question, the "theological-political
problem" has remained "*the* theme" of his investigations.
The question of the one thing needful induces him to come
to grips ever anew with the answers as well as the claims
of theology and politics: to come to grips with the *answers*
because political philosophy has to seek the quarrel over
what is right and may not flee confrontation with the alternatives if political philosophy is fully to develop its own power
and strength in the attempt to answer the question of the
order of human things coherently and comprehensively; and
to come to grips with the *claims* because political philosophy
always was and must be *political* philosophy, too, i.e. political
action in the service of philosophy, protection and defense

110. *To understand Socrates* is the central task that Strauss sets for himself in
Natural Right and History, and it is the unstated epigraph of his confrontation
with the two thinkers of modernity who exerted the strongest influence on him,
namely Nietzsche and Heidegger (*Natural Right and History* [Chicago, 1953]; cf.
the initial words, set off with capitals, of the Introduction and of chapters 3 and
4). "The problem of Socrates" is present in each of the fourteen books that
Strauss wrote after 1932. Nowhere is it expressed as urgently and as unconven-
tionally as in Strauss's late works: *Socrates and Aristophanes* (New York, 1966);
Xenophon's Socratic Discourse (Ithaca, 1970); *Xenophon's Socrates* (Ithaca, 1972).
111. Preface to the English translation of *Spinoza's Critique of Religion*, p. 31;
reprinted in *Liberalism Ancient and Modern*, p. 257. See—in addition to this long
preface of 1962, of which Strauss says in a letter to Alexandre Kojève that "it
comes as close to an autobiography as is possible within the limits of propriety"
(May 29, 1962, Leo Strauss Papers, Box 4, Folder 11)—the German preface to
Hobbes' politische Wissenschaft, pp. 7–8, and "A Giving of Accounts," in *The College
of St. John's, Annapolis*, vol. 22, no. 1 (April 1970), pp. 2–4; further, "An Unspoken Prologue to a Public Lecture at St. John's," in *Interpretation, A Journal of
Political Philosophy*, vol. 7, no. 3 (September 1978), p. 2.

of the philosophic life.[112] Politics and religion deserve the special attention of political philosophy not although but, rather, *because* politics is not everything and *because* not everything is faith. —Whereas the political does have central significance for the thought of Leo Strauss, the enemy and enmity do not. Enmity does not touch the core of his existence, and his identity does not take its shape in battle with the enemy. The friends that Strauss chose for himself tell us much more about his identity, and it becomes visible nowhere else than in his philosophy.

112. Reflection on the "art of careful writing," the rediscovery and revival of which in our century is connected to the name of Leo Strauss, has a prime place in this context. Toward the characterization of the politics of the philosophers, a statement about Alfarabi may be cited, by means of which Strauss's own politics is especially well described. This statement occurs in the Introduction to *Persecution and the Art of Writing* (p. 17) and reads: "We may say that Fārābā's Plato eventually replaces the philosopher-king who rules openly in the virtuous city, by the secret kingship of the philosopher who, being 'a perfect man' precisely because he is an 'investigator,' lives privately as a member of an imperfect society which he tries to humanize within the limits of the possible. Fārābā's remarks on Plato's policy define the general character of the activity of the *falāsifa*." In the Preface, Strauss gives the reader a hint that has no counterpart in all his other work: "For the Introduction I have made free use of my article 'Fārābā's *Plato*' (*Louis Ginzberg Jubilee Volume*, American Academy for Jewish Research, New York, 1945, 357–393)." The essay to which Strauss refers is one of his most important and one of the most helpful for the understanding of his philosophic project. The cited passage reads (p. 384): "We may say that Fârâbî's Plato replaces Socrates' philosopher-king who rules openly in the perfect city by the secret kingship of the philosopher who lives privately as a member of an imperfect community. That kingship is exercised by means of an exoteric teaching which, while not too flagrantly contradicting the accepted opinions, undermines them in such a way as to guide the potential philosophers toward the truth. Fârâbî's remarks on Plato's own policy define the general character of all literary productions of 'the philosophers.'" Though "philosophic politics" (*On Tyranny*, pp. 220–21) may stand in the foreground for the practice of the exoteric-esoteric way of writing, the "art of careful writing" has its deepest foundation not in the political but in the philosophical intention of those who make use of that art. That foundation cannot be perceived in the light of the *polemios*. Access is disclosed solely by *eros*. (*Persecution and the Art of Writing*, p. 36; *What Is Political Philosophy?* p. 40; *Thoughts on Machiavelli* [Glencoe, IL, 1958], p. 299; *Liberalism Ancient and Modern*, p. 8.)

Leo Strauss

NOTES ON CARL SCHMITT,
THE CONCEPT OF THE POLITICAL

I

[1] The treatise by Schmitt[1] serves the question of the "order of the human things" (95), that is, the question of the state. In view of the fact that in the present age the state has become more questionable than it has been for centuries or more (23 f.), understanding the state requires a radical foundation, "a simple and elementary presentation" of what the basis of the state is, which means the basis of the political; for "the concept of the state presupposes the concept of the political" (20).

[2] This thesis, with which the investigation of the concept of the political is begun, must be understood in accordance with Schmitt's own general principles of understanding. Following these principles, the sentence "the political precedes the state" can manifest the desire to express not an eternal truth but only a present truth. For "all spirit [is] only spirit of the present" (79); "all concepts of the spiritual sphere, including the concept of spirit, are in themselves pluralistic and are to be understood only in terms of their concrete political existence" (84); "all political concepts, ideas, and words [have] a polemical meaning; they have a concrete opposition in view, they are tied to a concrete situation . . ." (31). In accordance with these principles, it must be asked: To what extent does the present situation compel us to recognize that the basis of the state is the political? Against what opponent does the political emerge as the basis of the state?

---

1. *Der Begriff des Politischen. Mit einer Rede über das Zeitalter der Neutralisierungen und Entpolitisierungen neu herausgegeben von Carl Schmitt* (Munich and Leipzig, 1932). The parenthetical page numbers identify page numbers of that text. [Those numbers have been replaced in this translation by the page numbers of the 1963 edition.—H.M.]

[3] The present situation is characterized by the fact that a process three hundred years old has "reached its end" (94). The age at the end of which we find ourselves is "the age of neutralizations and depoliticizations." Depoliticization not only is the accidental or even necessary result of the modern development but is its original and authentic goal; the movement in which the modern spirit has gained its greatest efficacy, liberalism, is characterized precisely by the *negation* of the political (68 ff.). If liberalism has already become implausible, if it accordingly must be countered by "another system," then the first word against liberalism must in any case be: the *position* of the political. And if liberalism believed that by means of its negation of the political it could bring about the foundation of the state or, more accurately, the establishment of rational social relations, after the failure of liberalism one cannot help thinking that the state can be understood only from the position of the political. Thus Schmitt's basic thesis is entirely dependent upon the polemic against liberalism; it is to be understood only qua polemical, only "in terms of concrete political existence."

[4] Schmitt's task is determined by the fact that liberalism has failed. The circumstances of this failure are as follows: Liberalism negated the political; yet liberalism has not thereby eliminated the political from the face of the earth but only has hidden it; liberalism has led to politics' being engaged in by means of an antipolitical mode of discourse. Liberalism has thus killed not the political but only understanding of the political, sincerity regarding the political (65 ff.). In order to remove the smokescreen over reality that liberalism produces, the political must be made apparent as such and as simply undeniable. The political must first be brought out of the concealment into which liberalism has cast it, so that the question of the state can be seriously put.

[5] It is thus insufficient to establish as a fact that liberalism has failed, to show how liberalism drives itself ad absurdum in every political action, to indicate "that all good observers . . . despaired of finding here [in liberalism] any political principle or intellectual consistency" (69). Nor does it suffice to attain the insight that the manifest inconsistency of all liberal politics is the necessary consequence of the fundamental negation of the political (69). What is needed rather is to replace the "astonishingly consistent systematics of liberal *thought*," which is manifest within the inconsistency of liberal *politics*, by "another system" (70), namely, a system that does not negate the political but brings it into recognition.

[6] Schmitt is aware that the "astonishingly consistent . . . systematics of liberal thought" has, "despite all setbacks, still not been replaced in Europe today by any other system" (70), and this awareness alone suffices to characterize the significance of his efforts; for with this awareness he stands wholly alone among the opponents of liberalism, who usually carry an elaborate unliberal doctrine in their pocket. In making this observation Schmitt points to the basic difficulty of his own investigation also. For if it is true that the "systematics of liberal thought" has "still not been replaced in Europe today by any other system," it is to be expected that he, too, will be compelled to make use of elements of liberal thought in the presentation of his views. The tentativeness of Schmitt's statements results from that compulsion. Schmitt himself explicitly says so: he wants to do no more than "'*to delimit*' theoretically an immense problem"; the theses of his text "are conceived as a *point of departure* for an objective discussion" (96). The foregoing engenders the critic's duty to pay more attention to what distinguishes Schmitt from the prevailing view than to the respects in which he merely follows the prevailing view.

II

[7] Schmitt expressly desists from providing an "exhaustive definition" of the political (26). From the outset he understands the question of the *"essence* of the political" (20) as the question of *what is specific to* the political (21 and 26 f.). He does so, to be sure, not because he regards the question of the genus (within which the specific difference of the political has to be stipulated) as already answered or even as immaterial, but precisely because of his deep suspicion of what is today the most obvious answer: he pioneers a path to an original answer to the genus question by using the phenomenon of the political to push the most obvious answer ad absurdum. What is still today, despite all challenges, the most obvious, genuinely liberal answer to the question of the genus within which the peculiarity of the political and, therewith, of the state is to be defined is that this genus is *"culture,"* that is, the totality of "human thought and action," which is divided into "various, relatively independent domains" (26), into "provinces of culture" (Natorp). Schmitt would remain within the horizon of this answer if, as at first appears, he were to say: just as "in the domain of the moral the ultimate distinctions are good and evil, in the aesthetic domain beautiful and ugly, in the economic domain useful and harmful," so the "specifically political distinction . . . is the distinction between friend and enemy" (26). However, this ordering of the political next to, and equivalent to, the other "provinces of culture" is expressly rejected: the distinction between friend and enemy is *"not equivalent and analogous* . . . to those other distinctions"; the political does *not* describe "a new *domain* of its own" (27). What is hereby said is that the understanding of the political implies a

fundamental critique of at least the prevailing concept of culture.

[8] Schmitt does not express this critique everywhere. He too, using the terminology of a whole literature, occasionally speaks of the "various, relatively independent domains of human thought and action" (26) or of the various "spheres of human life and thought" (66). In one passage (71) he expresses himself in such a way that a superficial reader could get the following impression: after liberalism has brought the autonomy of the aesthetic, of morals, of science, of the economy, etc. into recognition, Schmitt now seeks, for his part, to bring the autonomy of the political into recognition, in opposition to liberalism but nonetheless in continuation of liberal aspirations for autonomy. To be sure, the quotation marks that he places around the word "autonomy" in the expression "autonomy of the various domains of human life" already show how little the foregoing is Schmitt's opinion. This [indication] becomes clearer when he emphasizes the "*matter-of-factness*" with which liberalism "not only recognizes the 'autonomy' of the various domains of human life but exaggerates it to the point of specialization and even to complete isolation" (71). Schmitt's aloofness from the prevailing concept of culture becomes fully clear in the following indirect characterization of the aesthetic: "the path from the metaphysical and the moral to the economic traverses the aesthetic, and the path across aesthetic consumption and enjoyment, be they ever so sublime, is the surest and most comfortable path to the universal economization of spiritual life . . ." (83); for the prevailing concept of culture surely includes recognition of the autonomous value of the aesthetic—assuming that this concept is not altogether constituted precisely by that recognition. This observation leads at least to the de-

mand that the prevailing concept of culture be replaced by another concept of culture. And that replacement will have to be based on the insight into what is specific to the political.

[9] Schmitt expressly forgoes, as we have seen, an "exhaustive definition" of the political. Proceeding on the assumption that the "various, relatively independent domains of human thought and action" (the moral, the aesthetic, the economic, etc.) have "their own criteria" by which they are constituted in their relative independence, he asks about the "criterion of the political." The criteria in question have the character of "ultimate distinctions," or, more accurately, of ultimate "oppositions." Thus the criterion of the moral is the opposition of good and evil, the criterion of the aesthetic, the opposition of beautiful and ugly, etc. In taking his bearings by this general relationship, Schmitt defines "the distinction between friend and enemy" as "the specifically political distinction" (26 f.). Here "enemy"—and thus also "friend"—is always to be understood only as the *public* enemy (friend), "a *totality* of men that fights at least potentially, that is, has a real possibility of fighting, and stands in opposition to a corresponding totality" (29). Of the two elements of the friend-enemy mode of viewing things, the "enemy" element manifestly takes precedence, as is already shown by the fact that when Schmitt explains this viewpoint in detail, he actually speaks only of the meaning of "enemy" (cf. 27, 29, and 32 f.). One may say: every "totality of men" looks around for friends only—it *has* friends only—because it already has enemies; "the essence of political relationships [is] contained in reference to a concrete *opposition*" (30). "Enemy" therefore takes precedence over "friend," because "the potential for a fight that exists in the region of the real" belongs "to the concept of the enemy"—and

not already to the concept of the friend as such (33), and "man's life" gains "its specifically *political* tension" from the potential for war, from the "dire emergency," from the "most extreme possibility" (35). But the possibility of war does not merely constitute the political as such; war is not merely "the most extreme political measure"; war is the dire emergency not merely within an "autonomous" region—the region of the political—but for man simply, because war has and retains a "relationship to the real possibility of *physical killing*" (33); this orientation, which is constitutive of the political, shows that the political is *fundamental* and not a "relatively independent domain" alongside others. The political is the "authoritative" (39). It is in this sense that we are to understand the remark that the political is "not equivalent and analogous" to the moral, the aesthetic, the economic, etc. (26).

[10] This definition of the political has the closest connection to Schmitt's suggested critique of the prevailing concept of culture. This critique questions the "autonomy" of the various "domains of human thought and action." Following the prevailing concept of culture, however, not only are the individual "provinces of culture" "autonomous" in relation to one another, but, prior to them, culture as a whole is already "autonomous," the sovereign creation, the "pure product" of the human spirit. This viewpoint makes us forget that "culture" always presupposes something that is cultivated: culture is always the *culture of nature*. This expression means, primarily, that culture develops the natural predisposition; it is the careful nurture of nature—whether of the soil or of the human spirit makes no difference; it thus *obeys* the orders that nature itself gives. But the statement can also mean *conquering* nature through obedience to nature (*parendo vincere*, in Bacon's phrase); then culture is not so much the faith-

ful nurture of nature as a harsh and cunning fight *against* nature. Whether culture is understood as the nurture of nature or as a fight with nature depends on how nature is understood: as exemplary order or as disorder to be eliminated. But however culture is understood, "culture" is certainly the culture of nature. "Culture" is to such an extent the culture of nature that culture can be understood as a sovereign creation of the spirit only if the nature being cultivated has been presupposed to be the *opposite* of spirit, and been *forgotten*. Because we now understand by "culture" primarily the culture of *human* nature, the presupposition of culture is primarily human nature; and because man is by his nature an *animal sociale*, the human nature on which culture is based is the natural social relations of men, that is, the way in which man, prior to all culture, behaves toward other men. The term for natural social relations understood in this manner is *status naturalis*. One can therefore say: the foundation of culture is the *status naturalis*.

[11] *Hobbes* understood the *status civilis* in the sense of the specifically modern concept of culture—here let it remain an open question whether, strictly speaking, there is any concept of culture other than the *modern* one—as the *opposite* of the *status naturalis;* the *status civilis* is the presupposition of every culture in the narrow sense (i.e. every nurture of the arts and sciences) and is itself already based on a particular culture, namely, on a disciplining of the human will. We will here disregard Hobbes's view of the relationship between *status naturalis* and culture (in the broadest sense) as an opposition; here we only emphasize the fact that Hobbes describes the *status naturalis* as the *status belli*, simply, although it must be borne in mind that "the nature of war, consisteth *not in actual fighting;* but in the known *disposition* thereto" (*Leviathan* XIII). In Schmitt's terminology this statement means that the *status*

naturalis is the genuinely *political* status; for, also according to Schmitt, "the political" is found "*not in fighting itself* . . . but in a behavior that is determined by this real *possibility*" (37). It follows that the political that Schmitt brings to bear as fundamental is the "state of nature" that underlies every culture; Schmitt restores the Hobbesian concept of the state of nature to a place of honor (see 59). Therewith the question about the genus within which the specific difference of the political is to be stipulated has also been answered: the political is a *status* of man; indeed, the political is *the* status as the "natural," the fundamental and extreme, status of man.

[12] To be sure, the state of nature is defined by Schmitt in a fundamentally different fashion than it is by Hobbes. For Hobbes, it is the state of war of individuals; for Schmitt, it is the state of war of groups (especially of nations). For Hobbes, in the state of nature everyone is the enemy of everyone else; for Schmitt, all political behavior is oriented toward *friend* and enemy. This difference has its basis in the *polemical* intention of Hobbes's definition of the state of nature: for the fact that the state of nature is the state of war of all against all is supposed to motivate the abandonment of the state of nature. To this negation of the state of nature or of the political, Schmitt opposes the position of the political.

[13] Granted, in Hobbes there is no question of a total negation of the political; according to his doctrine, the state of nature continues at least in the relationship between the nations. And thus Hobbes's polemic against the state of nature as the state of war of *individuals*—which Schmitt implicitly adopts, as shown by his comment, expressly following Hobbes, on the relationship between protection and obedience (53; cf. also 46 f.)—does not need to question the political in Schmitt's sense, that is, the "natural" char-

acter of the relationships of human *groups*. Nevertheless, according to Schmitt it belongs to the essence of the political group that it can "demand . . . from the members of its own nation *the readiness to die*" (46); and the justification of this claim is at least qualified by Hobbes: in battle he who deserts the ranks out of fear for his life acts "only" dishonorably, but not unjustly (*Lev.* XXI). The state can justifiably demand from the individual only *conditional* obedience, namely an obedience that does not stand in contradiction to the salvation or preservation of the life of this individual; for the securing of life is the ultimate basis of the state. Therefore, while man is otherwise obliged to unconditional obedience, he is under no obligation to risk his life; for death is the greatest evil. Hobbes does not shrink from the consequence and expressly denies the status of courage as a virtue (*De homine* XIII 9). The same attitude is disclosed in his definition of the *salus populi:* the *salus populi* consists (1) in defense against the enemy from without; (2) in preservation of peace within; (3) in just and modest enrichment of the individual, which is much more readily attained through work and frugality than through victorious wars, and is particularly promoted by the nurture of mechanics and mathematics; (4) in the enjoyment of innocuous freedom (*De cive* XIII 6 and 14). As soon as "humanity" becomes the subject or object of planning, these principles have to lead to the ideal of civilization, that is, to the demand for rational social relations of humanity as *one* "partnership in consumption and production" (58). Hobbes, to a much higher degree than Bacon, for example, is the author of the ideal of civilization. By this very fact he is the founder of liberalism. The right to the securing of life pure and simple—and this right sums up Hobbes's natural right—has fully the character of an inalienable human right, that is, of an individual's *claim* that takes precedence over the state and determines its purpose and its limits; Hobbes's foundation for the natural-right claim to the securing of life pure and simple sets the path to the whole system of human rights in the sense of liberalism, if his foundation does not actually make such a course necessary. Hobbes differs from developed liberalism only, but certainly, by his knowing and seeing *against what* the liberal ideal of civilization has to be persistently fought for: not merely against rotten institutions, against the evil will of a ruling class, but against the natural evil of man; in an unliberal world Hobbes forges ahead to lay the foundation of liberalism against the—*sit venia verbo*—unliberal nature of man, whereas later men, ignorant of their premises and goals, trust in the original goodness (based on God's creation and providence) of human nature or, on the basis of natural-scientific neutrality, nurse hopes for an improvement of nature, hopes unjustified by man's experience of himself. Hobbes, *in view of* the state of nature, attempts to overcome the state of nature within the limits in which it allows of being overcome, whereas later men either dream up a state of nature or, on the basis of a supposed deeper insight into history and therewith into the essence of man, forget the state of nature. But—in all fairness to later men—ultimately that dreaming and that oblivion are merely the consequence of the negation of the state of nature, merely the consequence of the position of civilization introduced by Hobbes.

[14]   If it is true that the final self-awareness of liberalism is the philosophy of culture, we may say in summary that liberalism, sheltered by and engrossed in a world of culture, forgets the foundation of culture, the state of nature, that is, human nature in its dangerousness and endangeredness. Schmitt returns, contrary to liberalism, to its author, Hobbes, in order to strike at the root of liberalism

in Hobbes's express negation of the state of nature.[2] Whereas Hobbes in an unliberal world accomplishes the founding of liberalism, Schmitt in a liberal world undertakes the critique of liberalism.

2. In the first edition of this treatise Schmitt had described Hobbes as "by far the greatest and perhaps the sole truly systematic political thinker" (*Archiv für Sozialwissenschaft und Sozialpolitik*, vol. 58, p. 25). Schmitt now speaks of Hobbes only as "a great and truly systematic political thinker" (64). In truth Hobbes is *the* antipolitical thinker ("political" understood in Schmitt's sense).

III

[15]   Schmitt confronts the liberal negation of the political with the position of the political, that is, with the recognition of the reality of the political. For the position of the political it is immaterial, in Schmitt's express opinion, whether one regards the political as desirable or detestable: the intent of the position "is neither bellicose or militarist, nor imperialist, nor pacifist" (33). Schmitt desires only to know *what is.* This statement does not mean that he considers his expositions "value-free," that he wants (whether out of concern for the scientific character of his study or for the freedom of personal decision) to leave open all possibilities for taking an evaluative stance toward the political. Rather, he intends precisely to seal off all such possibilities: the political *cannot* be evaluated at all, cannot be measured by an ideal; applied to the political, *all* ideals are nothing but "abstractions," *all* "normative prescriptions" nothing but "fictions" (49 f. and 28 f.). For the political is constituted by reference "to the real possibility of physical killing" of men by men (33); and "there is no rational purpose, no norm however correct, no program however exemplary, no social ideal however beautiful, no legitimacy or legality that can justify men's killing one another for its own sake" (49 f.).

[16]   The position of the political results in the *unpolemical* description of the political. As such, the position opposes Hobbes's polemical description of the state of nature. Hobbes had presented the state of nature as in itself impossible: the state of nature is the state of war of all against all; in the state of nature, everyone is the enemy of everyone else. According to Schmitt, the subjects of the state of nature are not individuals but totalities; furthermore, not every totality is the enemy of every other totality,

but alongside the possibility of enmity the possibilities of alliance and neutrality also exist (35). The state of nature so understood is in itself *possible*. That it is *real*, however, is proved by the whole history of humanity up to the present day. It may be that there will someday be a completely depoliticized state of humanity—"whether and when this state of the earth and of humanity will occur, I do not know"; at any rate that state "for the time being does not exist," and therefore it would be "a dishonest fiction to assume that it is at hand" (54).

[17]   Now one cannot—least of all can Schmitt himself—take relief in the fact that the depoliticized state *"for the time being* does not exist" (54), that "war as a real possibility is *still* present *today*" (37). In view of the fact that there is today a powerful movement striving for the total elimination of the real possibility of war and hence the abolition of the political, in view of the fact that this movement not only exercises a great influence upon the mentality of the age but also authoritatively determines the real circumstances—this movement led, after all, to war's being *"today* . . . probably neither something pious, nor something morally good, nor something profitable" (36), whereas in earlier centuries war could indeed be all these things—in view of this fact one must look beyond today and ask: granted that "war as a real possibility is still present today," will war still be a possibility present tomorrow? or the day after tomorrow? In other words: though the abolition of the political may in no way have succeeded *so far*, is not this abolition nevertheless possible in the future? is it not possible at all?

[18]   Schmitt gives the following answer to this question: The political is a basic characteristic of human life; politics in this sense *is* destiny; therefore man cannot escape politics (36 f., 66 f., 76 ff.). The inescapability of the

political is displayed in the contradiction in which man necessarily becomes entangled if he attempts to eliminate the political. This effort has a prospect of success if and only if it becomes political; that is, if it "is strong enough to group men into friends and enemies," if it thus "would be able to drive the pacifists into *war* against the nonpacifists, into a 'war against war.'" The war against war will then be undertaken as "the definitively final war of humanity." Such a war, however, is "necessarily especially intensive and inhuman" because in it the enemy is fought as "an inhuman monster . . . that must be not only fended off but definitively annihilated" (37). But humanity cannot be expected to be especially humane and, therefore, unpolitical after having just put behind it an especially inhumane war. Thus the effort to abolish the political for the sake of humanity has as its necessary consequence nothing other than the increase of inhumanity. When it is said that the political is a basic characteristic of human life, in other words that man ceases to be man if he ceases to be political, this statement also, and precisely, means that man ceases to be human when he ceases to be political. If man thus gets entangled in contradictions when he attempts to eliminate the political, that attempt is ultimately possible only through dishonesty: "To curse war as the murder of men, and then to demand of men that—so that there will 'never again be war'—they wage war and kill and allow themselves to be killed in war, is a manifest fraud" (49).

[19] The political is thus not only possible but also real; and not only real but also necessary. It is necessary because it is given in human nature. Therefore the opposition between the negation and the position of the political can be traced back to a quarrel over human nature. The ultimate controversy is whether man is by nature good or evil. Here, however, "good" and "evil" are "not to be

taken in a specifically moral or ethical sense"; rather, "good" is to be understood as "undangerous," and "evil" as "dangerous." Thus the ultimate question is "whether man is a dangerous or an undangerous being, a perilous or a harmless, nonperilous being" (59). "All genuine political theories" presuppose man's dangerousness (61). Accordingly, the thesis of man's dangerousness is the ultimate presupposition of the position of the political.

[20] The train of thought just recounted is in all probability not Schmitt's last word, and it is certainly not the most profound thing that he has to say. It conceals a reflection that moves in an entirely different direction, a reflection that cannot be reconciled with the line of thought described above.

[21] Schmitt describes the thesis of the dangerousness of man as the ultimate presupposition of the position of the political: the necessity of the political is as certain as man's dangerousness. But is man's dangerousness unshakably certain? Schmitt himself qualifies the thesis of man's dangerousness as a "*supposition*," as an "anthropological confession of *faith*" (58). But if man's dangerousness is only supposed or believed in, not genuinely known, the opposite, too, can be regarded as possible, and the attempt to eliminate man's dangerousness (which until now has always really existed) can be put into practice. If man's dangerousness is only believed in, it is in principle *threatened*, and therewith the political is threatened also.

[22] Schmitt concedes that the political is in principle threatened when he says: "Whether and when this [completely apolitical] state of the earth and of humanity will occur, *I do not know*" (54). Now the political could not be threatened if, as Schmitt asserts in a series of passages, it were simply inescapable. One must therefore add an obvious qualifier to his assertion that the political is inescap-

able, and must understand that assertion as follows: The political is inescapable as long as there is just *one* political opposition, even just as a possibility. Schmitt implies this qualifier in the course of the previously adduced argument against pacifism, for that line of argument presupposes that the opposition between pacifists and nonpacifists does not disappear. The inescapability of the political thus exists only conditionally; ultimately, the political remains threatened.

[23] If the political is ultimately threatened, the position of the political must ultimately be *more* than the recognition of the reality of the political, namely, an espousal of the threatened political, an *affirmation* of the political. It is therefore necessary to ask: why does Schmitt affirm the political?

[24] The political is threatened insofar as man's dangerousness is threatened. Therefore the affirmation of the political is the affirmation of man's dangerousness. How should this affirmation be understood? Should it be intended *politically*, it can have "no normative meaning but only an existential meaning" (49), like everything political. One then will have to ask: in time of danger, in the "dire emergency," does "a fighting totality of men" affirm the dangerousness of its enemy? does it *wish* for dangerous enemies? And one will have to answer "no," along the lines of C. Fabricius's comment when he heard that a Greek philosopher had proclaimed pleasure as the greatest good: If only Pyrrhus and the Samnites shared this philosopher's opinion as long as we are at war with them! Likewise, a nation in danger wants its own dangerousness not for the sake of dangerousness, but for the sake of being rescued from danger. Thus, the affirmation of dangerousness as such has no political meaning but only a "normative," *moral* meaning; expressed appropriately, that affirmation is

the affirmation of power as the power that forms states, of *virtù* in Machiavelli's sense. Here, too, we recall Hobbes, who describes fearfulness as the virtue (which, incidentally, is just as much negated by him as is the state of nature itself) of the state of nature, but who understands fearfulness as inclusive of glory and courage. Thus warlike morals seem to be the ultimate legitimation for Schmitt's affirmation of the political, and the opposition between the negation and the position of the political seems to coincide with the opposition between pacifist internationalism and bellicose nationalism.

[25]   Is that conclusion really correct? One has to doubt it if one considers the resolution with which Schmitt refuses to come on as a belligerent against the pacifists (33). And one must quarrel with the conclusion as soon as one has seen more precisely how Schmitt arrives at man's dangerousness as the ultimate presupposition of the position of the political. After he has aleady twice rejected the pacifist ideal on the ground that the ideal in any case has no meaning for behavior in the present situation and for the understanding of this situation (36 f. and 54 f.), Schmitt— while recognizing the possibility in principle of the "world state" as a wholly apolitical "partnership in consumption and production" of humanity united—finally asks "upon which men will the terrible power devolve that a global economic and technical centralization entails"; in other words, which men will *rule* in the "world state." "This question cannot by any means be dismissed by hoping . . . that government of men over men will have become superfluous, because men will then be absolutely free; for the question immediately arises, *for what* they will be free. One can answer this question with optimistic or pessimistic suppositions," namely with the optimistic supposition that man will then be undangerous, or with the pessimistic sup-

position that he will be dangerous (58 f.). The question of man's dangerousness or undangerousness thus surfaces in view of the question whether the government of men over men is, or will be, necessary or superfluous. Accordingly, dangerousness means *need of dominion.* And the ultimate quarrel occurs not between bellicosity and pacifism (or nationalism and internationalism) but between the "*authoritarian* and *anarchistic* theories" (60).

[26] The quarrel between the authoritarian and the anarchistic theories concerns whether man is by nature evil or good. But "evil" and "good," here, are "*not* to be taken in a specifically *moral* or ethical sense" but are to be understood as "dangerous" and "undangerous." What is thereby said becomes clear if one takes into account the double meaning of "evil" that Schmitt mentions. "'Evil' can appear as corruption, weakness, cowardice, stupidity, *but also* as 'coarseness,' instinctual drivenness, vitality, irrationality, etc." (59). "Evil," in other words, can be understood either as *human inferiority* or as *animal power*, as *humana impotentia* or as *naturae potentia* (Spinoza, *Eth.* III *praef.*). Now if "evil" is not meant in the moral sense, only the second meaning can be in question here. In this sense "the philosophers of statecraft of the seventeenth century (Hobbes, Spinoza, Pufendorff)" have described man in the state of nature as "evil": that is, "evil" "like *beasts* that are moved by their drives (hunger, cupidity, fear, jealousy)" (59). But the question arises *why* these philosophers, Hobbes in particular, understood man as "evil like the beasts." Hobbes had to understand evil as *innocent* "evil" because he denied sin; and he had to deny sin because he did not recognize any primary obligation of man that takes precedence over every claim *qua* justified claim, because he understood man as by nature free, that is, without obligation; for Hobbes, therefore, the fundamental political fact was

natural right as the justified *claim* of the individual, and Hobbes conceived of obligation as a *subsequent* restriction upon that claim. If one takes this approach, one cannot demur in principle against the proclamation of human rights as claims of the individuals upon the state and contrary to the state, against the distinction between society and state, against liberalism—assuming that liberalism is not altogether the unavoidable consequence of the Hobbesian approach. And once one understands man's evil as the innocent "evil" of the beast, but of a beast that can become astute through injury and thus can be educated, the limits one sets for education finally become a matter of mere *"supposition"*—whether very narrow limits, as set by Hobbes himself, who therefore became an adherent of absolute monarchy; or broader limits such as those of liberalism; or whether one imagines education as capable of just about everything, as anarchism does. The opposition between evil and good loses its keen edge, it loses its very meaning, as soon as evil is understood as innocent "evil" and thereby goodness is understood as an aspect of evil itself. The task therefore arises—for purposes of the radical critique of liberalism that Schmitt strives for—of nullifying the view of human evil as animal and thus innocent evil, and to return to the view of human evil as moral baseness; only in this way can Schmitt remain in harmony with himself if indeed "the core of the political idea" is "the *morally* demanding decision" (*Politische Theologie* 56). The correction that Schmitt undertakes in the view of evil held by Hobbes and his successors not only fails to meet the foregoing requirement but even contradicts it. Whereas in the case of Hobbes the natural and thus innocent "evil" is emphasized so that it can be *combated*, Schmitt speaks with an unmistakable *sympathy* of the "evil" that is not to be understood morally. This sympathy, however, is nothing other than *admiration* of animal power; and the same thing that Schmitt says in an already quoted passage on the aesthetic in general also applies to this admiration. Moreover, the inappropriateness of this sympathy immediately becomes clear when we discover that *what* is admired is not an excellence but a deficiency, a need (namely a need of dominion). Man's dangerousness, revealed as a need of dominion, can appropriately be understood only as moral baseness. It must be recognized as such, but it cannot be affirmed. But then what is the meaning of the affirmation of the political?

[27] *Why* Schmitt affirms the political, and, first of all, *that* he *affirms* it and does not merely recognize it as real or necessary, is shown most clearly in his polemic against the ideal that corresponds to the negation of the political. Ultimately Schmitt by no means repudiates this ideal as utopian—he says, after all, that he does not know whether it cannot be realized—but he does abhor it. That Schmitt does not display his views in a moralizing fashion but endeavors to conceal them only makes his polemic the more effective. Let us listen to Schmitt himself!: "if . . . the distinction between friend and enemy ceases even as a mere possibility, there will only be a politics-free weltanschauung, culture, civilization, economy, morals, law, art, *entertainment*, etc., but there will be neither politics nor state" (54). We have emphasized the word "entertainment" because Schmitt does everything to make entertainment *nearly* disappear in a series of man's serious pursuits; above all, the "etc." that immediately follows "entertainment" glosses over the fact that "entertainment" is really the ultimate term in the series, its *finis ultimus*. Schmitt thus makes it clear: The opponents of the political may say what they will; they may appeal on behalf of their plan to the highest concerns of man; their good faith shall not

be denied; it is to be granted that weltanschauung, culture, etc., do not *have* to be entertainment, but they *can* become entertainment; on the other hand, it is impossible to mention politics and the state in the same breath as "entertainment"; politics and the state are the only *guarantee* against the world's becoming a world of entertainment; therefore, what the opponents of the political want is ultimately tantamount to the establishment of a world of entertainment, a world of amusement, a world without *seriousness*. "A definitively pacified globe," Schmitt says in an earlier passage, "would be a world without politics. In such a world there could be various, perhaps *very interesting*, oppositions and contrasts, competitions and intrigues of all kinds, but no opposition on the basis of which it could sensibly be demanded of men that they sacrifice their lives" (35 f.; emphasis mine). Here, too, what Schmitt concedes to the pacifists' ideal state of affairs, what he *finds striking* about it, is its capacity to be interesting and entertaining; here, too, he takes pains to hide the criticism contained in the observation "*perhaps* very interesting." He does not, of course, wish to call into doubt whether the world without politics is interesting: if he is convinced of anything, it is that the apolitical world is *very* interesting ("competitions and intrigues of all sorts"); the "perhaps" only questions, but certainly *does* question, whether this capacity to be interesting can claim the interest of a human being worthy of the name; the "perhaps" conceals and betrays Schmitt's *nausea* over this capacity to be interesting, which is only possible if man has forgotten what genuinely matters. It thus becomes clear why Schmitt rejects the ideal of pacifism (more fundamentally: of civilization), why he affirms the political: he affirms the political because he sees in the threatened status of the political a threat to the seriousness of human life. The affirmation of the political is ultimately nothing other than the affirmation of the moral.

[28] One reaches the same result if one looks more closely at Schmitt's description of the modern age as the age of depoliticization. With this description he certainly does *not* mean that in the nineteenth and twentieth centuries politics is to a lesser extent destiny than in the sixteenth and seventeenth centuries; today, no less than in earlier times, humanity is divided into "totalities that have a real possibility of fighting one another." A fundamental transformation has occurred, not in *the fact* that men quarrel but in *what* they quarrel *about*. What men quarrel about depends on what is considered important, authoritative. Different things are regarded as authoritative in different centuries: in the sixteenth century, theology was authoritative; in the seventeenth, metaphysics; in the eighteenth, morals; in the nineteenth, the economy; and in the twentieth, technology. Basically: in every century a different "domain" is the "central domain" (80–84). The political, because it has "no . . . domain of its own" (27), is never the "central domain." Whereas the "central domains" change, the political constantly remains destiny. But as *human* destiny the political is dependent upon what ultimately matters for man: "the state, too, [gets] its reality and power from the respective central domain, because the authoritative issues that groups, divided into friends and enemies, quarrel about are likewise determined by the authoritative domain" (86). The exact meaning of the depoliticization that is characteristic of the modern age can thus be discerned only if one understands which law rules in the "succession of changing central domains." This law is the "tendency toward neutralization," that is, the striving to gain a ground that "makes possible security, clarity, agreement,

and peace" (89). Agreement and peace here mean agreement and peace at all costs. In principle, however, it is always possible to reach agreement regarding the means to an end that is already fixed, whereas there is always quarreling over the ends themselves: we are always quarreling with each other and with ourselves only over the just and the good (Plato, *Euthyphro* 7B-D and *Phaedrus* 263A). Therefore, if one seeks agreement at all costs, there is no other path than to abandon entirely the question of what is right and to concern oneself solely with the means. It thus becomes intelligible that modern Europe, once it had started out—in order to avoid the quarrel over the right faith—in search of a neutral ground *as such*, finally arrived at faith in technology. "The self-evidence of today's widespread faith in technology is based only on the fact that people were able to believe that in technology they had found the absolutely and definitively neutral ground . . . In comparison to theological, metaphysical, moral, and even economic questions, which one can quarrel about forever, purely technical problems entail something refreshingly objective; they allow of solutions that are clear" (89–90). But the neutrality of technology is only apparent: "Technology always remains an instrument and a weapon, and precisely because technology serves everyone, it is not neutral" (90). The speciousness of this neutrality reveals the absurdity of the attempt to find an "absolutely and definitively neutral ground," to reach agreement at all costs. Agreement at all costs is possible only as agreement at the cost of the meaning of human life; for agreement at all costs is possible only if man has relinquished asking the question of what is right; and if man relinquishes that question, he relinquishes being a man. But if he seriously asks the question of what is right, the quarrel will be ignited (in view of "the inextricable set of problems" (90) this question entails), the life-and-death quarrel: the political—the grouping of humanity into friends and enemies—owes its legitimation to the seriousness of the question of what is right.

[29] The affirmation of the political is the affirmation of the state of nature. Schmitt opposes the affirmation of the state of nature to the Hobbesian negation of the state of nature. The state of nature is the *status belli,* pure and simple. Thus it appears that the affirmation of the state of nature can only be bellicose. That appearance fades away as soon as one has grasped what the return to the state of nature means for Schmitt. The affirmation of the state of nature does not mean the affirmation of war but "relinquishment of the security of the status quo" (93). Security is relinquished not because war would be something "ideal," but because it is necessary to return from "splendid vicarage," from the "comfort and ease of the existing status quo" to the "cultural or social nothing," to the "secret, humble beginning," "to undamaged, noncorrupt nature" (93) so that "out of the power of a pure and whole knowledge . . . the order of the human things" can arise again (95).

[30] If, then, according to Schmitt's actual opinion, the position of the political can be traced back to the position of the moral, how does that position square with the polemic, which pervades his whole text, against the primacy of morals over politics? The first explanation that suggests itself is that by "morals" in that polemic he is referring to altogether specific morals, namely, a morals that stands in fundamental contradiction to the political. For Schmitt, "moral"—at least as used in the context here—always refers to "*humanitarian* morality" (cf. 80 ff.). But that usage means that Schmitt is tying himself to his

opponents' view of morality instead of questioning the claim of humanitarian-pacifist morals to *be* morals; he remains trapped in the view that he is attacking.

[31] Now the polemic against morals—against "ideals" and "normative prescriptions"—does not prevent Schmitt from passing a *moral* judgment on humanitarian morals, on the ideal of pacifism. Of course, he takes pains, as we have shown, to conceal this judgment. An *aporia* finds expression in this concealment: the threatened status of the political makes necessary an evaluative statement on the political; yet at the same time insight into the essence of the political arouses doubt about all evaluative statements on the political. For such a statement would be a "free, unmonitorable decision that concerns no one other than the person who freely makes the decision"; it would essentially be a "private matter" (49); but the political is removed from all arbitrary, private discretion; it has the character of transprivate *obligation.* If it is now presupposed that all ideals are private and thus nonobligatory, obligation cannot be conceived as such, as duty, but can be conceived only as inescapable necessity. It is this presupposition, then, that disposes Schmitt to assert the inescapability of the political, and—as soon as his subject matter forces him to stop maintaining this assertion—to conceal his moral judgment; and this presupposition is, as he himself emphasizes, the characteristic presupposition of the "individualistic-liberal society" (49).

[32] Let us now make thoroughly clear what the affirmation of the political in disregard of the moral, the primacy of the political over the moral, would signify. Being political means being oriented to the "dire emergency." Therefore the affirmation of the political as such is the affirmation of fighting as such, wholly irrespective of *what* is being fought *for*. In other words: he who affirms the

political as such comports himself *neutrally* toward all groupings into friends and enemies. However much this neutrality may differ from the neutrality of the man who denies the political as such, he who affirms the political as such and thereby behaves neutrally toward all groupings into friends and enemies does not want "to place" himself "outside the political totality . . . and live only as a private man" (52); he does not have the *will* to neutralization, to the avoidance of decision at all costs, but in fact is eager for decision; as eagerness for *any* decision *regardless of content*, this neutrality makes use of the possibility—which originally was made accessible for the sake of neutralization—of something that is beyond all decision. He who affirms the political as such respects all who want to fight; he is just as *tolerant* as the liberals—but with the opposite intention: whereas the liberal respects and tolerates all *"honest"* convictions so long as they merely acknowledge the legal order, *peace*, as sacrosanct, he who affirms the political as such respects and tolerates all *"serious"* convictions, that is, all decisions oriented to the real possibility of *war*. Thus the affirmation of the political as such proves to be a liberalism with the opposite polarity. And therewith Schmitt's statement that "the astonishingly consistent . . . systematics of liberal thought" has "still not been replaced in Europe today by any other system" (70) proves to be true.

[33] The affirmation of the political as such can therefore be only Schmitt's first word against liberalism; that affirmation can only *prepare for* the radical critique of liberalism. In an earlier text Schmitt says of Donoso Cortés: he "despises the liberals, whereas he respects atheistic-anarchistic socialism as his mortal enemy . . ." (*Politische Theologie* 55). The battle occurs only between mortal enemies: with total disdain—hurling crude insults or maintaining the rules of politeness, depending on tempera-

ment—they shove aside the "neutral" who seeks to mediate, to maneuver, between them. "Disdain" is to be taken literally; they do not deign to notice the neutral;[TN7] each looks intently at his enemy; in order to gain a free line of fire, with a sweep of the hand they wave aside—without looking at—the neutral who lingers in the middle, interrupting the view of the enemy. The polemic against liberalism can therefore only signify a concomitant or preparatory action: it is meant to clear the field for the battle of decision between the "spirit of technicity," the "mass faith that inspires an antireligious, this-worldly activism" (93), and the opposite spirit and faith, which, as it seems, still has no name. Ultimately, two completely opposed answers to the question of what is right, confront each other, and these answers allow of no mediation and no neutrality (cf. the remark about "two-membered antitheses" and "three-membered diagrams" or "constructions" on p. 73). Thus what *ultimately* matters to Schmitt is not the battle against liberalism. For that very reason the affirmation of the political as such is not his last word. His last word is "the order of the human things" (95).

[34] It is nonetheless true that the polemic against liberalism very often seems to be Schmitt's last word, that he very often gets entangled in the polemic against liberalism, and that he thus gets diverted from his real intention and is detained on the level staked out by liberalism. This entanglement is no accidental failure but the necessary result of the principle that "all concepts of the spiritual sphere . . . are to be understood only in terms of concrete political existence" (84), and that "all political concepts, ideas, and words" have "a *polemical* meaning" (31). *In concreto* Schmitt violates this principle, which itself is entirely bound to liberal presuppositions, by opposing his unpolemical concept of the state of nature to Hobbes's polemical

concept of the state of nature; and he fundamentally rejects this principle by expecting to gain the order of human things from a *"pure and whole* knowledge" (95). For a pure and whole knowledge is never, unless by accident, polemical; and a pure and whole knowledge cannot be gained "from concrete political existence," from the situation of the age, but only by means of a return to the origin, to "undamaged, noncorrupt nature" (93).

[35] We said [par. 14 above] that Schmitt undertakes the critique of liberalism in a liberal world; and we meant thereby that his critique of liberalism occurs in the horizon of liberalism; his unliberal tendency is restrained by the still unvanquished "systematics of liberal thought." The critique introduced by Schmitt against liberalism can therefore be completed only if one succeeds in gaining a horizon beyond liberalism. In such a horizon Hobbes completed the foundation of liberalism. A radical critique of liberalism is thus possible only on the basis of an adequate understanding of Hobbes. To show what can be learned from Schmitt in order to achieve that urgent task was therefore the principal intention of our notes.

Editorial Note

Leo Strauss's "Notes on Carl Schmitt, *The Concept of the Political*" first appeared in the *Archiv für Sozialwissenschaft und Sozialpolitik* (Tübingen), vol. 67, no. 6 (August–September 1932), pp. 732–49. Leo Strauss republished them both as an appendix to his book *Hobbes' politische Wissenschaft* (Neuwied, 1965), pp. 161–81, and, in an English translation by E. M. Sinclair, as an appendix to the American edition of his 1930 book on Spinoza, *Spinoza's Critique of Religion* (New York, 1965), pp. 331–51. The Sinclair translation was included, with Strauss's permission in Carl Schmitt, *The Concept of the Political*; Translation, Introduction, and Notes by George Schwab; with Comments on Schmitt's Essay by Leo Strauss (New Brunswick, NJ, 1976), pp. 81–105.

My edition follows the first printing of 1932 in all details. Only printing errors were corrected. Deviations in Strauss's citations from the wording in Schmitt's text have been retained, unfootnoted (*gleichwertig* [equivalent] instead of *gleichartig* [homogeneous] in paragraphs 7 and 9; *moralisch anspruchsvolle Entscheidung* [morally demanding decision] instead of *anspruchsvolle moralische Entscheidung* [demanding moral decision] in paragraph 26; *nicht kontrollierbare* [unmonitorable] instead of *nichtkontrollierte* [unmonitored] in paragraph 31). On the other hand, all page references to the 1932 text of the *Concept of the Political* have been replaced by those of the 1963 reprint to enable the reader to locate without difficulty the passages Strauss cites and to pursue the references that he provides. For ease of citation, the paragraphs of the Strauss essay have been numbered.

Leo Strauss

THREE LETTERS TO CARL SCHMITT

Letter One

Hohenzollernkorso 11
Berlin-Neutempelhof
March 13, 1932

Dear Professor Schmitt:

The secretarial office of the Rockefeller Foundation
has now informed me that the Foundation's German
Committee has recommended me to the Paris Central Office in the way I had wished. The final confirmation is expected in mid-May. Given that this confirmation has, as I
hear, yet to be withheld in any instance, I can now presumably count on being sent to Paris in the autumn of
this year.

I cannot let the occasion of this communication pass
without assuring you once again of my most heartfelt
thanks for your support of my application. But it is not
only this help in an outward matter, albeit of nearly vital
importance, that compels my gratitude to you. Allow me,
Professor, to submit that the interest that you have
shown in my studies of Hobbes represents the most hon-
orable and obliging corroboration of my scholarly work
that has ever been bestowed upon me and that I could
ever dream of.

Respectfully yours,
Leo Strauss

Letter Two

Hohenzollernkorso 11
Berlin-Neutempelhof
September 4, 1932

Dear Professor Schmitt:

I have reflected once again in the past few days on the ideas you have expressed in your *Concept of the Political* and also on my objections, which have in the meantime been published in the *Archiv für Sozialwissenschaft*. In the course of those reflections, two points have occurred to me that I would like to report to you by letter because I can no longer present them in my review.

As far as I have seen from various conversations about your book, your thesis is particularly subject to misunderstandings because you occasionally express yourself more or less as follows: political opposition is the highest degree of intensity of all possible group oppositions. These formulations invite the misunderstanding that the political always presupposes the prior existence of human oppositions that in themselves have an unpolitical character, in other words that the political is something *subsequent or supplementary*. But if I have correctly understood your opinion—admittedly taken more from an oral exchange than from your text—it leads precisely to the conclusion that there is a *primary* tendency in human nature to form *exclusive groups*.

In attempting to analyze your text more thoroughly, one gets the impression that the polemic against the Left, a polemic that at first glance appears completely unified, collapses into two incompatible or at least heterogeneous lines of thought. The opposition between Left

and Right is presented (1) as the opposition between in-
ternationalist pacifism and bellicose nationalism and (2)
as the opposition between anarchistic and authoritarian society. No proof is needed to show that *in themselves* these
two oppositions do not coincide. In my review I have explained why the second opposition (anarchy versus authority) appears to me to be the more radical and, in the final
judgment, the only opposition that comes into consideration. But it goes without saying that one cannot rest
easy with the foregoing observation. After all, the coinci-
dence, at first merely empirical, of bellicose nationalism
and sympathy for authoritarian order can hardly be
wholly accidental. Does it accord with your understanding to explain the connection between "authoritarianism"
and "nationalism"—allow me for now these abbrevia-
tions—as follows: The ultimate foundation of the Right
is the principle of the natural evil of man; because man
is by nature evil, he therefore needs *dominion.* But dominion can be established, that is, men can be unified, only
in a unity *against*—against other men. Every association
of men is *necessarily* a separation from other men. The *ten-*
dency to separate (and therewith the grouping of humanity into friends and enemies) is given with human nature;
it is in this sense destiny, period. But the political thus
understood is not the constitutive principle of the state,
of "order," but only the condition of the state. Now this
relationship of rank between the political and the state
does not emerge sufficiently, I believe, in your text.
Your statement "The concept of the state presupposes
the concept of the political" is ambiguous: "presupposition" can mean constitutive principle *or* condition. In the
first sense the statement can hardly be maintained, as the
etymology (political-*polis*) already proves. The reviewer
of your text probably meant to make this objection in the

Rhein-Mainische Volkszeitung (July 5), when he charged you with "sociologism."

I close with the request that you take note of this supplement to my review with the same forbearance you show with respect to the review itself.

Respectfully yours,
Leo Strauss

Letter Three

4 rue du Parc de Montsouris
Paris (14e)
July 10, 1933

Dear Professor Schmitt:

First [I] would like to inform you that the Rockefeller Fellowship, which I essentially owe to your evaluation of the first part (submitted to you) of my studies on Hobbes, has now been awarded to me for a second year. I intend to study here for another semester and to go to England in the early part of next year.

Next I would like to respectfully request of you a piece of information. You related to me on one occasion that Professor Friedrich (of Harvard University) had informed you of a plan to prepare a critical edition of the works of Hobbes. I would be very interested in collaborating on that edition. I have sufficient experience in the technical aspects of editing, and, moreover, I will certainly have the opportunity during my stay in England to familiarize myself with the Hobbes manuscripts. I would be very obliged to you if you could let me know at your convenience what the chances are that the edition of Hobbes's works—I do not even know if all his writings or only the political writings would be involved—will materialize, and, further, whether you would be prepared to support my participation in this edition.

As for "Paris," I can scarcely report anything to you with which you would not already be familiar. Of the local scholars the Arabist Massignon and André Siegfried have made the strongest impression on me. Philosophy here is still, on the whole, at the prewar stage; the trea-

tises are in general, that is, on the average, more solid
than in Germany, which probably has something to do
with better humanistic education, on the average, in this
country.

Meanwhile I have been somewhat occupied with Maur-
ras. The parallels to Hobbes—one can probably not
speak of dependence—are striking. I would be very glad
if I could speak to him. Would you be in a position and
willing to write me a few lines by way of an introduction
to him? I should be deeply indebted to you if you could
do so.

Assuring you once again of my sincere thanks for the
support that you have given me, I remain

Respectfully yours,

Leo Strauss

Editorial Note

Letters I and III are in Leo Strauss's handwriting; letter II is typewritten and signed by Strauss. The originals are in the Nordrhein-Westfälisches Hauptstaatsarchiv Düsseldorf. Strauss kept a carbon copy of letter II, which today is part of the Leo Strauss Papers of the University of Chicago Library. I thank Professor Joseph Cropsey, literary executor of the estate of Leo Strauss, and Professor Joseph Kaiser, literary executor of the estate of Carl Schmitt, for permission to publish the letters. I include the adviser of the Carl Schmitt Archiv in Düsseldorf, Dr. Eberhard Freiherr von Medem, in my thanks for the cooperation that these helpful gentlemen have extended to me in my investigations.

No letters from Schmitt to Strauss could be discovered either in Chicago or in Düsseldorf. Schmitt apparently never answered the two questions that Strauss directed to him on July 10, 1933. On October 9, 1933, Strauss remarks in a letter to his friend Jacob Klein, who at that time still lived in Germany: "Do you know that Carl Schmitt . . . and . . . no longer answer letters? Is that generally the case now?" Klein answers on October 12, 1933: "Whether C. Schm. can answer at all is the question! I regard his present position as absolutely impossible. I do not know if you have the picture. Regarding that, too, I will write in my next letter, which I will not send via Germany." On October 21, Klein once more speaks of Schmitt: "Regarding C. S., it can be said that he is joining the crowd in an *inexcusable* way. In the official position he now holds, no doubt he *cannot* very well answer . . . And I would certainly not write to him again." Karl Löwith writes Strauss on December 6, 1933, from Marburg (the letter from Strauss to which Löwith refers is not extant): "Dr. [Werner]

Becker [a student of Schmitt's and author of a dissertation on Hobbes], to whom I spoke today, regards it as out of the question that Schmitt—despite his anti-Semitism in principle—has not answered you *for that reason* . . . but (1) he has an enormous amount of work to do as *Staatsrat* and (2) Becker says that Schmitt also would know of no English Hobbes scholar to whom one could be recommended."

Schmitt kept the letters from Strauss not among his general correspondence but in a special folder with the inscription "On the *Concept of the Political* 3 Important Pieces of Correspondence: 1. Leo Strauss [1929–] 1932–34, 2. Alexandre Kojève (1955), 3. Joachim Schickel [1970] 1968–70." (The dates "1929" and "1970" were corrected by hand by Schmitt. This information was provided by Dr. von Medem.) Schmitt showed the letters to various visitors and apprised me of them several months before his death. By his account, Strauss was still writing to Schmitt "from England in 1934." So far, according to Dr. von Medem, no letter from England, where Strauss *was* living in 1934, can be found among Schmitt's literary remains. If there was a 1934 letter from Strauss—if Schmitt's memory was correct and the inscription on the folder was not based on a mere oversight—it is very likely that Strauss expressed criticism in that letter. On October 10, 1934, he writes to Jacob Klein in Berlin: "Have you seen Carl Schmitt's last pamphlet [clearly meaning *Über die drei Arten des rechtswissenschaftlichen Denkens*]? He is now against the decisionism of Hobbes and for 'thinking in terms of order' on the basis of the arguments in my review, which of course he does not cite. I will perhaps inform Koellreutter about that." Klein answers on October 13, 1934: "I urgently advise you not to correspond with Koellreutter about that. Here there is only one thing: absolute silence." In a letter to E. I. J. Rosenthal (May 10, 1935), Strauss concedes that Schmitt, because he "meanwhile had become a National Socialist," could "adduce the mitigating circumstance that after all he could not possibly allow himself to acknowledge his dependence on a Jew." (Dr. George Elliott Tucker, general editor of the *Independent Journal of Philosophy*, Paris, afforded me access to the letters to Jacob Klein. The other letters are in the Department of Special Collections, the University of Chicago Library, Leo Strauss Papers, Box 2, Folder 6; Box 2, Folder 11; and Box 4, Folder 16.)

TRANSLATOR'S NOTES
(designated in the text by "TN1, TN2," etc.)

1. *Ernstfall* does not allow of any altogether felicitous translation. The noun *Ernst* means seriousness. *Ernstfall* refers to a state of emergency in which everything important is at stake, a matter of life and death. In this translation, *Ernstfall* is always rendered by "the dire emergency." The emergency can be a military emergency or a civil war but can also be an individual's dire emergency, quite apart from the state or community.

2. The infamous *Reichsstatthaltergesetz* provided each of the German states (*Länder*) with standing representatives of the central government in Berlin. By means of this law the National Socialists intended to strengthen the central power of the state and to compel strict toeing of the party line throughout Germany.

3. The German for "figure" is *Gestalt*. "Form," which we sometimes use, would make for a smoother translation here, but Schmitt's use of *Gestalt* in a certain context is sometimes intentionally eccentric. Cf. especially "The enemy is our own question as a figure" in n. 103 above.

4. "In point of fact, the end of human Time or History—that is, the definitive annihilation of Man properly so-called or of the free and historical Individual—means quite simply the cessation of Action in the full sense of the term. Practically, this means: the disappearance of wars and bloody revolutions. And also the disappearance of *Philosophy;* for since Man himself no longer changes essentially, there is no longer any reason to change the (true) principles which are at the basis of his [knowledge] of the World and of himself. But all the rest can be preserved indefinitely; art, love, play, etc., etc.; in short, everything that makes Man *happy*." English text taken from the second edition of the

James H. Nichols Jr. translation, *Introduction to the Reading of Hegel* (Ithaca and London: Cornell University Press, 1980), p. 159.

5. *'Leib'haftigkeit*. Depending on the context, *der Leibhaftige* can be another name for the Devil.

6. In order to make sense of this curious expression, it helps to know that the source is Max Stirner, a spokesman for nihilism: *"Ich hab' Mein Sach' auf Nichts gestellt."* (*Der Einzige und sein Eigentum* [Leipzig, 1845], opening sentence.)

7. "Disdain" here translates *Verachtung*, and the etymologically related "do not deign to notice" translates *achten nicht*.

INDEX

Printed and bound by CPI Group (UK) Ltd, Croydon, CR0 4YY

09/06/2025

14685704-0002